DRAGONS OF
DELTORA

ISLE OF
THE DEAD

D0058028

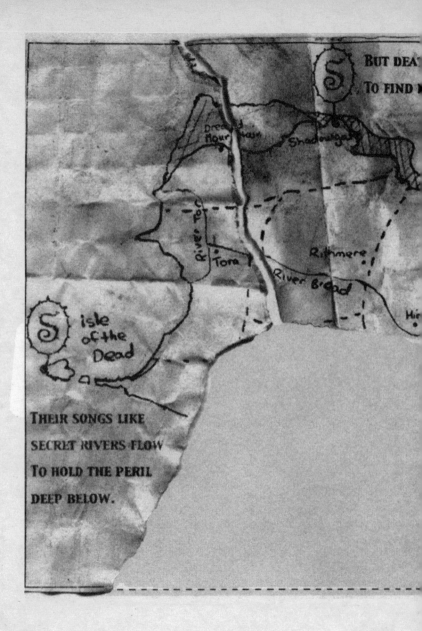

BUT DEAT[...]
TO FIND [...]

Dread
Moor

Shadowga[...]

River To[...]
Tora

Rithmere

River Bro[...]

Hir[...]

isle
of the
Dead

THEIR SONGS LIKE
SECRET RIVERS FLOW
TO HOLD THE PERIL
DEEP BELOW.

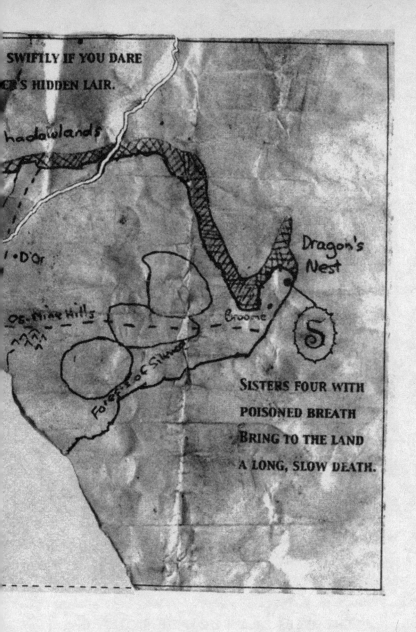

SWIFTLY IF YOU DARE

...R'S HIDDEN LAIR.

...hadowlands

Dragon's
Nest

•D'Or

...os Nine Hills

Forest of Silus

Broone

S

SISTERS FOUR WITH
POISONED BREATH
BRING TO THE LAND
A LONG, SLOW DEATH.

A land of magic and monsters . . .

DRAGONS OF DELTORA

#1 DRAGON'S NEST
#2 SHADOWGATE
#3 ISLE OF THE DEAD

DELTORA SHADOWLANDS

#1 CAVERN OF THE FEAR
#2 THE ISLE OF ILLUSION
#3 THE SHADOWLANDS

DELTORA QUEST

#1 THE FORESTS OF SILENCE
#2 THE LAKE OF TEARS
#3 CITY OF THE RATS
#4 THE SHIFTING SANDS
#5 DREAD MOUNTAIN
#6 THE MAZE OF THE BEAST
#7 THE VALLEY OF THE LOST
#8 RETURN TO DEL

THE DELTORA BOOK OF MONSTERS

DRAGONS OF
DELTORA

ISLE OF
THE DEAD

EMILY RODDA

SCHOLASTIC INC.

New York   Toronto   London   Auckland   Sydney
Mexico City   New Delhi   Hong Kong   Buenos Aires

for Reuben Jakeman

No part of this publication may be reproduced, or stored in a retrieval system or transmitted in any form or by any means, electronic, mechanical, photocopying, recording, or otherwise, without written permission of the publisher. For information regarding permission, write to Permissions Department, Scholastic Australia, PO Box 579, Lindfield, New South Wales, Australia 2070.

ISBN 0-439-63375-3

Text and graphics copyright © Emily Rodda, 2004.
Graphics by Kate Rowe.
Cover illustrations copyright © Scholastic Australia, 2004.
Cover illustrations by Marc McBride.

All rights reserved. Published by Scholastic Inc., 557 Broadway, New York, NY 10012, by arrangement with Scholastic Press, an imprint of Scholastic Australia.

SCHOLASTIC and associated logos are trademarks and/or registered trademarks of Scholastic Inc.

12 11 10 9 8 7 6 5 4   5 6 7 8 9/0

Printed in the U.S.A.   40
First American edition, December 2004

Contents

The story so far . . .

Lief, Barda, and Jasmine are on a secret quest to find and destroy the Four Sisters, Shadow Lord creations that are poisoning Deltora. To succeed, they must wake Deltora's last seven dragons, which have been deep in enchanted sleep for centuries. Only when the power of a dragon joins with the power of a gem in the Belt of Deltora can a Sister be destroyed.

Deltora's dragons, fierce protectors of their land, were hunted almost to extinction by the Shadow Lord's Ak-Baba. When only one dragon from each gem territory remained, the explorer Doran the Dragonlover persuaded them to sleep in safety until a king, wearing the Belt of Deltora, called them to wake.

Too late, Doran learned of the Shadow Lord's plan to use the Four Sisters to starve Deltora's people. Once the dragons had gone there was nothing to stop the Enemy from putting the Sisters in place. Doran tried to warn of the danger, but was not believed. Leaving a map showing where he thought the Sisters were, he set out to find proof. He never returned, and his map was marked by the Shadow Lord, torn into four parts, and hidden.

The first map fragment led Lief, Barda, and Jasmine to Dragon's Nest, where, with the ruby dragon, they destroyed the Sister of the East and found a second map part pointing to Shadowgate in the north. Despite the efforts of the evil Laughing Jack, they reached Shadowgate, destroyed the Sis-

ter of the North with the emerald dragon, and found the third part of the map.

Now they must move on to seek the Sister of the West on the fearful Isle of the Dead.

Now read on . . .

1 - The Chase

Doom strolled through the great doorway of the palace in Del, and casually scanned the northern sky. He saw the messenger bird the guards had reported, but his stern, scarred face showed no sign of eagerness, fear, or hope.

Many people were talking on the stairs that led down to the palace lawn and the road beyond. There was much to talk about. For weeks there had been rumors of strange happenings in the east — of dragons flying the skies and crops beginning to thrive.

Now the same tales had begun coming in from the north.

But none of the people on the stairs approached Doom to ask him if the rumors were true. None of them did more than glance nervously at the silent figure by the palace doors. Doom was a legend among them, but they feared him.

1

With all their hearts they wished their young king would return from his tour around the kingdom. Times were hard, and they missed Lief sorely.

The bird swooped down and dropped its message into Doom's hands. To the disappointment of the people turning to look, Doom moved inside at once. Whatever the message was, he plainly did not intend to share it.

✳

Alone in the palace dining room, Doom tore open the message with a feverish haste that would have very much surprised those who thought he had no feelings.

Sea serpents swim north
in rippling well wet boats
all sail.

Fish news fin more slippery
gills bring flippers will ocean
friend water old shellfish.

Whales west foaming waves
moving tides are fishbones
we hook.

Tonight seaweed city scales
white shore.

The note was not signed, but the familiar writing told Doom that Lief, at least, was safe. A tiny piece of brown wood had been folded within the paper. Doom picked it up and smelled it.

"Boolong cone," he muttered, raising his eyebrows. "So — he is on Dread Mountain. And the others?"

He glanced at the sketch at the top of the note, then read each sentence from back to front, leaving out all words that had anything to do with fish.

All well in north. His heart gave a great thud. This could only mean that against all odds the Sister of the North had been destroyed, and that Lief, Barda, and Jasmine were all safe.

Old friend will bring more news. Gla-Thon of the Dread Gnomes, perhaps. There was no one else Doom could think of who might have helped the companions in the north.

We are moving west. So they had found the third fragment of the map of Doran the Dragonlover. They knew the location of the Sister of the West!

White city tonight. At this, Doom leaped to his feet. Tora! Lief, Barda, and Jasmine would be in the marble city of magic this very night! No doubt they were going to ask the Torans to speed them to their new goal. A message sent now would reach them just in time.

Hastily he scribbled a note, then strode into the hallway and turned in the direction of the guarded area where the messenger birds were kept.

As he reached the library he remembered with a stab of irritation that old Josef the librarian wished desperately to write to Lief. His nagging had nearly driven Doom mad over the past weeks.

The library door was open. Inside, Josef's assistant Paff was arranging books on shelves, looking even more harried than usual.

"Where is Josef?" Doom demanded.

Paff jumped, and her pink-rimmed eyes widened. "He — is in the kitchen," she said breathlessly. "He did not eat at midday because — "

"Run to him at once, if you please," Doom broke in impatiently. "A bird is leaving with a message for Lief very soon. This is Josef's chance to send a note, if he makes haste. Take paper and a pen for him."

"Josef always carries a pen and a notebook with him," Paff said, then waited, her mouth hanging slightly open.

"Go then!" Doom thundered.

Paff dropped the books she was holding, shot past him like a startled rabbit, and ran in the direction of the kitchen.

Doom moved on, his face like thunder. In truth, he was annoyed with himself for losing his temper with someone as defenseless as Paff. But the people he passed drew back fearfully, and wished all the more that their beloved Lief would come home.

❋

While Doom was striding through the palace and Josef was dropping his soup spoon and frantically searching for his little notebook, Lief was flying towards Tora in the pouch of a Kin.

A few days before, he, Barda, and Jasmine had been astounded when three of the fabled flying creatures had arrived in Shadowgate to carry them to rest and safety on Dread Mountain.

The Kin were Ailsa, Bruna, and young Prin. Prin had grown very much since the companions last saw her and was now almost as large as Ailsa.

"But — how did you know where we were?" Lief had gasped when the first joyous greetings were over.

"Dreaming Water!" Prin said proudly. "Every night for weeks I have drunk the Water and thought of you, so I could visit you in my dreams."

"We have all been so afraid for you," sighed Bruna. "The Dread Gnomes, too — especially your good friend Gla-Thon. She wanted to speed to your aid when you first arrived in Shadowgate, but the old leader Fa-Glin forbade it. He said that if you had wanted Gla-Thon's help, you would have asked for it."

Stunned, Lief exchanged glances with Barda and Jasmine. So their whereabouts had not been secret at all — on Dread Mountain, at least!

"Let us fly!" Prin squeaked. "Everyone is wild to

see you. The Gnomes are trying to make a welcome feast. But how can they make a feast when they have no food but a few old berries and stalks?"

"They should learn to eat Boolong cones, as we do," said Bruna. "There are very many of those."

Lief, Barda, and Jasmine had said no more. But during the next few days, while they rested in the caverns of the Gnomes, and the famous green moss from the Dread Mountain stream healed Lief's wounds, they had talked and wondered a great deal.

Somehow the Shadow Lord had always known where they were in the north. They had not been able to understand why. Perhaps they now had their answer.

Trust only old friends . . .

So Doom had said in his last message. And the Dread Gnomes were old friends, just as the Kin were. But were all the Gnomes of the same mind? Or was there one whose loyalty lay in the Shadowlands?

It would only take one . . .

They told only Gla-Thon of their fears.

"Much as I wish to, I cannot swear there is no traitor among us," she said soberly. "There can be one bad berry in any bunch, however sweet it seems."

And so it was that the companions smilingly put their fingers to their lips when any question about their future travels was asked of them in the caverns of the Gnomes.

So it was that they sent no message to Del until

Gla-Thon could arrange for a bird to fly in secret, the day they left Dread Mountain.

So it was that they asked the Kin to give them all that remained of the Dreaming Water, knowing that the gentle creatures could refuse them nothing.

And so it was that they asked Ailsa, Bruna, and Prin to carry them away, but did not tell them where they were to go until they were high in the air and no one else could hear.

Careful and suspicious people themselves, the Gnomes accepted without complaint the companions' desire for secrecy. Fa-Glin also supplied all manner of goods to help them on their way — including a soft leather bag filled with gold pieces, which Jasmine had tucked securely in one of her many pockets.

"It is nothing," Fa-Glin had sighed when they thanked him. "Gold and jewels we have in plenty. If only we could eat them!"

Now the Kin were flying towards Tora, skimming over the low hills that rolled beyond the mountains. The light was slowly dimming and the wind was blowing across their path, but Lief, Barda, and Jasmine were all sure they would reach their goal by nightfall.

Then suddenly Kree, who was flying beside them, wheeled and screeched. And behind them they heard a distant, furious roar.

They turned their heads and saw a large green shape streaking towards them from the mountains.

Lief felt a thrill of fear. The emerald dragon had joined him to destroy the Sister of the North, but he knew that it felt no friendship towards him. And by the sound of its roars, it was very angry.

Filli squealed and bolted into hiding beneath Jasmine's collar. Bruna and Ailsa screamed, and their wingbeats faltered. But Prin put down her head and made an abrupt right turn.

"Prin, come back!" Ailsa shrieked after her. "You are going the wrong way! You are flying towards the coast!"

"Do you wish to be eaten?" cried Prin. "That is a dragon, Ailsa! A dragon! We can never outfly it unless we use the wind."

"If we can cross the border into amethyst country, it will not be able to follow!" Lief shouted. "Do your best!"

With the wind at their backs, the Kin made good speed. The hills beneath them gave way to flat, barren land, and soon they could see the glittering sea ahead. But every moment the dragon was gaining on them.

We must have crossed the border long ago, Lief thought in dismay. *But it has not stopped — if anything, it is flying faster!*

And suddenly Kree was crying a warning and the beast was above them, bearing down on them, forcing them to the ground.

Sobbing with fright, the Kin thudded to land.

Lief, Barda, and Jasmine rolled from their pouches and at once were pinned down by the wind of the dragon's mighty wingbeats.

Then, abruptly, they could move again, and the pounding of the waves and the cries of seabirds were the only sounds they could hear.

Shakily they crawled to their feet. The dragon was crouching beside them, huge and menacing. Its green eyes blazed with anger. The spines on its back were like quivering spears.

"Do you dare to steal the emerald away yet again from its territory and mine, young king?" it hissed.

Lief felt Barda and Jasmine move behind him, and knew that they were reaching for their weapons, poised to defend him. But his hands remained on the Belt of Deltora. He knew he must show no sign of weakness.

"I must take it, dragon of the emerald," he said. "It is part of the Belt that unites us all. And I must wear the Belt to the Isle of the Dead, in the land of the diamond, to find and destroy the Sister of the West."

"What do I care for the Sister of the West?" hissed the dragon. "The evil in my land is gone, and that is all that matters."

Lief took a deep breath. "The man you called Dragonfriend — the man known to us as Doran the Dragonlover — did not agree with you," he said.

The dragon did not blink. But at the mention of Doran's name a stillness settled over it. Lief knew that he had its attention.

"Doran thought as I do about our land," he went on firmly. "Your territory is all that matters to you, perhaps. But for Doran, the whole of Deltora was important."

He took a deep breath and met the dragon's eyes unflinchingly.

"Doran lost his life because he tried to find the Four Sisters and foil the Shadow Lord's plans," he said. "Now we are risking *our* lives to finish the work he began. You must not hinder us. You must let us go!"

2 ~ Bone Point

Slowly the fire in the green eyes died and the wicked spines were lowered. "You speak to me as plainly as Dragonfriend spoke long ago when he persuaded me to sleep," the dragon growled. "And though I do not like it, I accept your words, as once I accepted his."

The relief was so great that Lief almost staggered.

"Thank you," he said. "Then we will go on our way."

"If you must," the dragon said coldly. "But I warn you — beware the dragons of the amethyst and the diamond. Emerald dragons are honorable. Others are full of lies and hungry for land and power."

Lief made no reply. He knew it was useless to argue. Jasmine, however, was not so wise.

"You are a fine one to talk of honor, dragon," she

snapped. "You crossed the border into amethyst territory without a thought when you were pursuing us! Yet when the lapis-lazuli dragon entered *your* land, you — "

The dragon bared its fangs. "Do not speak of that small, sly beast to me, girl! If it invades my territory again, I will tear it apart. Its blood will wash my stones. Its scales will fall on my mountains like rain."

"Why, you dragons hate your own kind even more than you hate the Shadow Lord!" Jasmine exclaimed. "I cannot think how Doran persuaded you to trust one another enough to sleep — even to save your lives!"

Steam gushed from the dragon's jaws. "I did not trust the other dragons," it hissed furiously. "I trusted Dragonfriend, whom I loved, and who knew my true name. Your foolishness angers me. I bid you farewell."

With a dull clatter it unfurled its leathery wings.

Kree took flight with a squawk, the Kin cowered, and Lief, Barda, and Jasmine scrambled clear.

The next moment, they were again pinned to the ground by the gale of huge wingbeats. And when at last they were able to raise their heads, the dragon was far above them, a shadow in the dimming sky.

"Jasmine!" cried Lief in exasperation.

"I merely spoke the truth." Jasmine shrugged, as Kree fluttered back to her arm.

"Speaking of truth," Barda said, "I fear it is true to say that we are in a pretty pickle. Look around you."

Jasmine and Lief turned and looked.

They were on a long point of land stretching out into the sea. A narrow road wound to the land's end, where a lighthouse rose, tall, white, and lonely. Wind whistled across the flat earth, bringing with it the sting of salt. Waves crashed against the rocks. A few seabirds wheeled above the foam-flecked ocean, their cries faint and ghostly.

"This is a dreary place, indeed," Jasmine said. Filli whimpered under her collar. All that could be seen of him was the tip of his nose.

"It would help if we knew where we were, Lief," Barda muttered. "You have the map — "

"We do not need the map," Lief said slowly.

His companions glanced at him in surprise.

"I know of this place," Lief went on, staring at the lighthouse. "It is called Bone Point."

"Well, whatever its name is, it is as flat as gnomes' bread," scowled Prin. "We cannot take flight from here. We should never have let ourselves be forced down. Now we are stranded!"

"Better stranded than torn to pieces in the air!" snapped Ailsa.

Barda jerked his head towards the tall white column of the lighthouse. "The lighthouse has a viewing platform at the top. Surely you could take off from there?"

"We could try," said Ailsa doubtfully.

Lief made a small movement, as if he was about to protest. When Barda glanced at him, however, he pressed his lips together and nodded.

"Yes. We have no choice," he muttered. "Even if the amethyst dragon senses the Belt and comes to us, it will not be able to carry us all."

He squared his shoulders and began walking swiftly towards the lighthouse.

※

When Jasmine and Barda at last caught up with Lief, he was standing by the lighthouse door, staring up at the viewing platform. Protected by bright red railings, the platform circled the tall building like a necklace. Above it gleamed the windows of the light chamber, neatly capped by a rounded red roof.

Barda exclaimed in surprise and pointed to an engraved stone set into the base of the lighthouse wall:

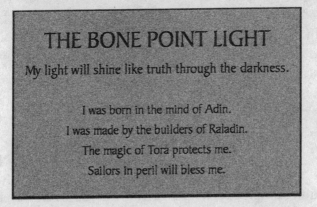

THE BONE POINT LIGHT

My light will shine like truth through the darkness.

I was born in the mind of Adin.
I was made by the builders of Raladin.
The magic of Tora protects me.
Sailors in peril will bless me.

"Yes, the great Adin arranged for the lighthouse to be built," Lief said, glancing down at the stone. "It was just after he united the seven tribes and became king. This verse is printed in the *Deltora Annals*. Josef showed it to Mother and me, just before she left for the west."

"Why, it looks as new as if it was completed only yesterday!" Barda said.

" 'The magic of Tora protects me . . .' " Jasmine read, and frowned in puzzlement.

"Bone Point was part of the territory of the Toran tribe," Lief said slowly. "And, as we know only too well, the magic of the ancient Torans was very powerful."

His companions nodded, remembering the disaster that had befallen the present people of Tora when they broke their ancestors' magic oath of loyalty to Adin and his heirs. Their years of exile from their city had ended only when Lief, as king, forgave them for their fault in Adin's name.

"Adin asked the ancient Torans to protect the Light," Lief went on. "He feared that the Shadow Lord might plot to destroy it. It suited the Enemy for Deltora to be isolated — for foreign ships to stay away."

"So — the Light signalled welcome to people from lands to our west?" asked Jasmine.

"It did welcome them, no doubt. But its real purpose was to act as a guide and warning," Lief said. "A hidden spine of rock spears into the sea from the tip of Bone Point. It has been the death of many ships that ventured too near it in the darkness of the night."

In silence they all turned to look at the sea.

"The tide is coming in," Barda murmured.

Waves crashed hard on the tip of the point, and to the south of the lighthouse. But on the northern side, close to where they were standing, there was a sheltered bay. Shells littered the bay's smooth half-moon of pale sand. Higher up, the faded remains of a small red boat lay almost buried in mounds of dry seaweed.

"Fish may not be plentiful, but surely it is still worth throwing out a line when food is so scarce." Barda frowned. "What is the lighthouse keeper thinking of, to let his boat go to ruin?"

"There is no lighthouse keeper," Lief said. "Red Han, the man who kept the Bone Point Light in my father's time, was the last. The Light has been dark since the Shadow Lord invaded and the Torans were banished from their city."

"But what of the foreign ships?" Jasmine asked.

"No foreign ships come near us now," Lief said. "Perhaps because of the danger. Perhaps because the people to our west take the darkness as a sign that the Shadow Lord still rules in Deltora. We do not know."

"But the Torans are back in their city now!" Barda exclaimed. "Surely the Light can be made to shine again? And surely another lighthouse keeper can be found? It is lonely work, I daresay, but — "

"It is not that," Lief broke in wearily. "It is something far more strange."

He paused, then met his companions' curious eyes and went on reluctantly.

"Part of the spell the ancient Torans cast was that only the keeper of the Light, the one sworn to protect it, could enter the chamber where it burned. If a keeper became ill, or wearied of the task, he or she was bound to travel to Tora and solemnly resign before all the people. Only then could a new keeper be appointed."

"A foolhardy spell indeed," Barda said grimly.

Lief grimaced. "So it seems. But no doubt it did not seem so dangerous in the time of Adin. The ancient Torans were very sure of their power. And for many centuries all was well."

He sighed. "But eighteen years ago, something

happened at Bone Point. We do not know what it was. All we know is that the Light went out, and Red Han disappeared."

"No doubt he was easy prey for Ols or Gray Guards once the Torans had been swept away, and their magic no longer protected him," Jasmine said.

"No doubt," Lief answered. "And the sudden loss of both the light keeper and the magic of Tora explains only too well why the Light went out."

"Then why — ?" Barda began impatiently.

"Do you not see?" Lief exclaimed. "Red Han never resigned his trust! The light chamber is sealed. The ancient spell still holds. And it cannot be broken — even by the present people of Tora."

"But — " Jasmine frowned. "But — this must mean that Red Han is still alive, for surely his death would break the spell. Why has he not returned?"

"Because he was unworthy of the trust placed in him!" growled Barda. "He broke his oath and ran away when the protection of Tora was lost. And now he skulks in some corner of Deltora, afraid to come out of hiding."

Lief shook his head, frowning. "Zeean of Tora knew Red Han. She says he was a simple man, but a man of good faith. He had been the light keeper at Bone Point for twenty years. She does not believe he would have betrayed his trust."

"But he could not have resigned in the proper way, even if he wanted to, Lief!" Jasmine exclaimed.

"From what you say, by the time he left here, Tora was deserted."

"That does not explain why he is missing to this day," Lief said. "And it does not explain — "

He broke off, and glanced over his shoulder. The Kin were still some distance away, toiling along the road on their short, stubby legs.

"All those who have entered the lighthouse feel — wickedness," he went on in a low voice. "They hear sounds and see things that are not there. Many say that the place is haunted."

Barda snorted. "Wind howls around a lighthouse. Birds cry and the sea pounds. Add to that a room that cannot be entered and a tale of a missing lighthouse keeper, and timid folk might easily imagine ghosts."

"Perhaps," Lief said. "But my mother is far from timid. She has been here, with Zeean of Tora. Both of them saw things that could not be explained. Bone Point has been a place of ill-omen in these parts for a long time, Barda. No one will come near it."

Barda grinned. "Indeed?" he asked. "Well, plainly one soul at least is not afraid. Perhaps you should ask *her* to be the lighthouse keeper."

"Who?" Lief asked, looking around.

"Why, the girl on the shore!" Barda exclaimed. "The girl painting the — "

He turned again towards the little bay. His jaw dropped.

Puzzled, Lief and Jasmine followed his eyes. But there was nothing to see. The bay was utterly deserted.

"But — but she was there!" Barda gasped. "A girl — about Jasmine's age — with long red hair. She was painting a picture. She had an easel and a brush. She was wearing a yellow skirt. It was tossing in the wind. I — I saw her plainly! Where is she?"

He turned this way and that, searching the flat land frantically. But there was no sign of anyone, and no footprints marked the weed-strewn sand.

"I saw her!" he repeated stubbornly.

Lief nodded. "I am sure you did," he said. "Red Han did not live here alone. And he was not the only one to disappear. Red Han had a daughter."

3 - The Lighthouse

Barda stood stiff with shock. He opened his mouth, but before he could speak, Filli popped his head out from beneath Jasmine's jacket and began chattering a welcome. Prin was panting up to the lighthouse with Bruna and Ailsa close behind her.

"What are you looking for, Barda?" Prin asked. "Have you lost something?"

Barda turned like one in a dream. "Only my senses, it seems," he mumbled.

Plainly he was going to say no more, so Prin turned her attention to the lighthouse.

"Oh, it is much larger than it looks from a distance!" she squealed. "And we can all fit through the door easily, I am sure of it! Shall I — ?"

"Wait!" Lief exclaimed. Gently he pushed Prin aside and put his hand on the shining brass doorknob.

"Jasmine and I will go in first," he said. "You Kin

follow, close behind us. Barda will come last. It is very important that we stay together. Do you understand?"

The three Kin nodded, their eyes wide.

"Is there . . . danger?" whispered Bruna, glancing worriedly at Prin.

"The lighthouse is deserted," Lief said carefully. "But we may see or hear things — things that are not real."

"Spirits!" Prin squeaked in excitement.

Bruna made a frightened sound and clasped her small front paws.

"Some say they are spirits," said Lief. "My mother says they are only visions from the past, kept alive by the walls of this place. The lighthouse is very old, and the magic of Tora is in every stone of it."

He sighed. "The builders of Raladin have been asked to try to knock it down so that another lighthouse can be built in its place. But the Torans have little hope that this can be done."

He turned the brass knob. The door opened smoothly, as though its hinges had been freshly oiled.

Inside it was very dark, and cold as death.

"Something bad happened here," quavered Prin, stepping back. "Something very bad. I feel it."

"I, too," Bruna murmured.

"And I," said Ailsa.

"We will turn back, if you wish," Lief said.

"No," said Ailsa in a small voice. "We will go on. Dreams cannot harm us."

Lief and Barda lit their lanterns. As the flames flared up and began to glow, they saw in front of them a spiral staircase winding upwards. Shadows flickered on smooth, curved stone walls.

Looking up, Lief thought he saw a flash of yellow, like the swirling hem of a yellow skirt. He caught his breath.

"It is not real," Jasmine murmured behind him. And he knew that she had seen what he had seen.

On the wall at the foot of the stairs hung a painting framed by polished sticks of driftwood. It was a picture of the little bay and the sea beyond, painted with love and skill.

The sea was glittering in early morning light. A red rowboat was drawn up on the smooth, wet sand, which was marked with a wavy line of shells cast up by the tide. At the bottom of the painting was a signature.

Verity

Lief reached out and touched the name gently with the tips of his fingers.

Bubbling laughter floated down the stairs. Lief jumped violently.

"Father!" a high, excited voice called, echoing,

echoing in the tall, hollow space. "A visitor is coming. Someone is rowing in from that ship! Go down to meet him, Father! Make haste!"

Bruna wailed softly.

"I have caught some fish, too!" the voice ran on. "And the water berries by the bay have ripened. Is it not wonderful? We will be able to give him a good dinner, if he will stay."

Visions from the past . . . Not real . . .

Mother, Zeean, and Peel saw only glimpses, and heard only muffled sounds, Lief thought. *They reported nothing like this.*

He touched the Belt of Deltora, hidden beneath his clothes. *The great amethyst, the gem of Tora, the symbol of truth, is in its own territory now*, he thought. *It feels the power in the lighthouse stones. I must expect that we will see and hear more than others have done.*

Gritting his teeth, he set his foot on the first stair and began to climb.

He climbed fast, trying to keep his mind blank, concentrating on the sound of his companions' footsteps close behind him.

Every now and then he would come to another painting fastened to the stone wall. There were paintings of seabirds, shells, the lighthouse from every angle, the sea in every mood. All had plainly been created by the same loving hand, and were signed in the same way. He took care not to touch them.

Verity, he thought. *A girl with red hair who loved*

the birds and the sea. A lighthouse keeper's daughter, who rowed in a little red boat, and fished, and painted pictures of what she saw around her. What happened to her? Why does her shade linger here?

He remembered what his mother had told him of Verity.

"Little was known of her except that she was born in the lighthouse," Sharn had said. "Her mother died when the girl was only one year old. The local folk say that she was raised by her father and the sea."

Lief realized that there was a door ahead of him. He climbed the last few steps and, holding his breath, pushed the door open. Holding the lantern high, he cautiously moved into the room beyond.

His companions crowded after him, the Kin squeezing through the doorway with grunts and groans.

Barda turned to close the door behind him. He stared.

"Certainly, something has happened here," he said. "This door is damaged. It looks as if it has been kicked. And these marks . . ."

He lowered his lantern and bent to peer at the ominous dark smears that stained the dented, splintered wood of the door.

Lief was looking around him. Plainly, they were in the lighthouse keeper's sitting room.

Dim light filtered through two round windows, one looking back to the land, one looking out to sea.

Many more paintings decorated the walls. Two easy chairs sat together in front of an old black stove. There was a bright woollen rug on the floor. There was a small table with wooden benches on either side of it, and a shelf stacked with blue-striped plates and cups.

It should have been a cozy scene, but it was not. Instead, the room chilled the blood. The very air seemed to taste of misery and horror.

On the far side of the room, near the stove, there was another door. Lief knew that beyond it must be a second staircase that led to the bedchambers and at last to the viewing platform.

Yet he could not make himself move. Nor, it seemed, could anyone else. They stood in silence, crowded together. No one was willing to take the first step.

A cold breeze brushed Lief's cheek. He caught a glimpse of movement from the corner of his eye.

He turned his head slowly. He blinked.

The room had been deserted only moments before. Now he could see, as if through a light mist, two men sitting on either side of the table, playing cards.

Cups stood at the men's elbows, and empty stone bottles lay in a jumble on the floor around their feet. The candle flickering between the men had burned down to a lumpy stub, swimming in wax.

Visions from the past . . .

Lief opened his dry lips. "Do you see them?" he whispered.

"Yes." His companions' voices were like the rustling of leaves in the wind. The Kin sounded terrified.

The man facing them had a broad face, dark red hair, and a bushy red beard. His blue eyes were bloodshot and deeply shadowed. His shoulders were bowed. His blunt fingers trembled as he threw down his cards.

"You win again," he said thickly. "It is nearly dawn. I — I will play no more."

The other man nodded.

He had his back to Lief. Lief could see nothing of him but a dark coat and limp black hair pushed behind a pair of large ears. But something about the way his narrow shoulders tensed showed that this was the moment he had been waiting for.

"Then pay me what you owe, Red Han," this man said softly. "And I will leave you."

"I cannot pay," the bearded man muttered. "You know it, Gant! Why, at midnight I told you I was ruined. You yourself urged me to play on, saying my luck was sure to change." He put his face in his hands. "Ah, what a fool I was to listen to you!" he groaned. "Instead of winning back what I had lost, I now owe three times the sum I owed before!"

"You had better keep your voice down, or you will wake your daughter," the man called Gant murmured. "Let her sleep while she can. She will find out what has happened soon enough."

The bearded man gave a muffled sob.

In one smooth movement, Gant drew a sheaf of papers from his pocket and put them on the table.

Lief, Barda, and Jasmine leaned forward and caught a glimpse of the top sheet.

PROMISE TO PAY

I ...... *Red Ham* ...... of
Bone Point
...... *Lighthouse* ......
owe the sum of ...*10 gold coins*...
to *Captain James Gant of The
Lady Luck.*

*By all I hold dear I swear to
pay my debt, and to seal my solemn
oath I make my mark below.*

Red Han

James Gant flicked through the papers with long, thin fingers.

"Why, it *has* been a long night, my poor fellow!" he said softly. "You have signed ten notes in all, I see. And each is for ten gold coins."

Red Han thrust his fingers through his hair and tugged as if to tear it out by the roots. "I cannot pay!" he repeated. "Where would I get a hundred gold coins?"

The thin man shook his head. "You should have thought of that before," he said regretfully. "You signed the notes. You swore a solemn oath to pay."

"It was madness!" groaned Red Han. "Madness!" He looked up, glaring at his visitor with haunted eyes. "You — you encouraged me! You filled out the notes and gave me them to sign. You made it so easy!"

His visitor shrugged. "I was merely trying to help," he said. He paused, then leaned forward, clasping his bony hands on top of the pile of papers.

"Perhaps — perhaps there is something I can do for you, even now," he said, raising his voice to a normal tone for the first time. "There is nothing I like better than helping those less fortunate than myself. Why, I *live* to do good. And you seem such a worthy fellow."

Lief went cold. Those words . . . that voice! He heard Jasmine draw a sharp breath and knew that she, too, had recognized them.

Why had he not seen it before? This vision from the past, this man calling himself Captain James Gant . . . was the man they knew as Laughing Jack.

4 - A Matter of Honor

Jasmine clutched Lief's arm. "Laughing Jack!" she breathed. "I did not know him! He reminded me of someone, certainly, but before he spoke I was racking my brains to think who it was. His hair . . ."

"He is younger," Lief whispered back. "At least eighteen years younger. What we are seeing happened before the Shadow Lord invaded. Red Han was still keeper, and the Light was still burning."

The lighthouse keeper's face had filled with hope. "You will forgive me my debt?" he exclaimed.

"Oh, no, I cannot do that," said his tormentor calmly. "It is a matter of honor — and of business, which is even more important. But . . . perhaps you could do me a service, in exchange for what you owe."

"Anything!" Red Han gasped. "Anything!"

"Excellent," purred Laughing Jack.

He bent forward and began to whisper, so low that Lief could not hear him.

Red Han's eyes widened. His hopeful expression faded, changing to a look of stunned horror.

"But why — why would you want such a thing of me?" he stammered. "If the Bone Point Light goes out, any ship that sails to this coast will be in danger. Foreign ships will stop visiting our shores."

"No doubt," said Laughing Jack.

Red Han leaned forward, his broad brow knotted. "But those ships come to trade," he said. "And more and more Deltora needs the food they offer in exchange for goods. I do not know why we cannot grow enough food for our own needs. But it is so. Would you have our people starve?"

The thin shoulders were raised in a shrug. "You need not concern yourself with such matters, Han," the soft voice said. "Think only of your debt, which must be paid. And bless the good fortune that made you the only one who can enter the chamber of the Bone Point Light."

Red Han's bloodshot eyes narrowed. "By the magic of Tora, that is true," he whispered. "But how do you know it?"

The next moment, he had leaped to his feet, overturning the bench, which crashed to the ground behind him.

"You are a servant of the Enemy!" he hissed. "You tricked me! You came here with one purpose, and one purpose only! To corrupt me and darken the Light. Snake! Traitor! Get out!"

The other man laughed. "And what of the debt you swore to pay? Swore by all you hold dear?"

"Hang the debt!" roared Red Han.

His visitor laughed again. "Ah, it is not so easy," he said softly. "You will pay. One way or another, you will pay."

Red Han lunged at him. With astonishing speed, Laughing Jack slipped from his bench and twisted aside. Han crashed into the second bench and fell.

The door to the second stairway flew open. A girl stood there, her eyes still blurry with sleep. A mass of curling red hair framed her startled face. A blue cloak had been hastily thrown over her nightgown.

"Father!" she cried, seeing her father on the ground and starting forward. "What has happened? Are you — "

"Verity, go back!" thundered her father, struggling to rise.

But it was too late. With the speed of a striking snake, Laughing Jack's long arm whipped around the girl's neck. In seconds she was pinned against his chest, the point of a knife pressed to her throat.

"One step and she dies, Red Han," snarled Laughing Jack. Dragging Verity with him, he began backing towards the door that led downstairs.

He was moving straight for Lief, Barda, Jasmine,

and the Kin. Barda reached out, but his hands clutched at empty air. Laughing Jack and his captive passed through the companions like a cold wind, leaving them shuddering, chilled to the bone.

The lighthouse keeper stood motionless by the table, his fists clenched, his eyes dark with terror.

"I had hoped we could settle this like gentlemen." Laughing Jack smiled. "I dislike crude violence. But you have forced my hand, lighthouse keeper. You have refused to perform the small service I asked of you in payment of your debt. So I will take what is my due — the thing you hold most dear."

"No," whispered Red Han. "No — I beg you!"

Laughing Jack smiled cruelly. "Then put out the Light," he said.

"What!" cried Verity in horror. "Father! No!"

Red Han's face was drawn with anguish. His voice trembled as he spoke.

"I will never put out the Light. I swore to defend it, whatever the cost. And so it must be."

Laughing Jack's lip curled. "Indeed!" he spat. "Then your daughter will pay the price."

"I am willing to pay it," the girl whispered. "I would rather die than — "

Her voice broke off in a choking sob as the bony arm tightened around her neck.

"From your tower you will have a good view of my ship, Red Han," Laughing Jack said softly, easing the door open. "Keep watch. Know that your daughter's suffering is on your own head. When you have seen enough and the Light goes out, Verity will be returned — in what condition, is up to you."

With that, he slipped through the door and slammed it after him. His footsteps rang on the stairs as he ran downwards.

Sick with rage and pity, Lief watched as Red Han sprang to the door with an anguished cry. Han twisted the knob, but the door would not open.

So Laughing Jack had some powers of sorcery, even then, Lief thought. *Not enough to break the spell set on the Light by the people of Tora. But enough for this.*

Red Han kicked the heavy wood and beat on it with his fists. The door shuddered, but held firm.

"Verity!" he groaned. Great tears were rolling down his cheeks. His fists had begun to bleed, but still he struck the door with all his strength.

"No more!" Lief heard Bruna wail.

And suddenly, the vision of Red Han trembled and was gone.

Stunned, the companions looked around. The table was again bare and empty, and the benches stood primly upright. Bruna's quiet sobbing was the only sound.

"So now we know why the Bone Point Light went out," Barda said heavily.

"No!" Jasmine was shaking her head. "Red Han was strong. And so was his daughter. Neither of them would have given in."

"Yet the Light *did* go out," said Lief. "And the food ships ceased to come, just as the Enemy planned."

"Let us leave here," Ailsa begged. "Ah, I was wrong to say that dreams cannot harm you. I am very sore in my heart."

Barda led the way across the room and flung open the second door. As they had expected, another spiral staircase was revealed.

"So I have seen Laughing Jack for myself after all," he muttered as they began to climb. "He is a nasty piece of work, and no mistake."

He frowned. "I am sure I have heard the name *The Lady Luck* before, long ago. I cannot think where, but no doubt it will come to me."

"It is strange to think that once Laughing Jack was the captain of a ship," said Jasmine thoughtfully.

"Very strange." Barda shook his head. "In my experience, people who work by or on the sea rarely move away from it. Yet Laughing Jack seems to have forsaken the coast for the inland."

"Perhaps he hates the memory of his wickedness here," Ailsa suggested quietly from behind them. "Perhaps he fled out of shame."

"No," said Jasmine shortly. "He has no shame. More likely he had to give up his ship because his crew mutinied and ran away from his cruelty. If only the poor beasts he forces to draw his wagon could do the same!"

Lief was behind her, so he could not see her face. But he could hear the pain in her voice.

Briefly he wondered at it. Jasmine's years surviving alone in the Forests of Silence had taught her that life was often cruel. When she could not change a thing, she normally accepted it and moved on, her mind fixed firmly on the future. Yet plainly the memory of Laughing Jack's horses still stabbed her like a knife.

They reached a landing with two open doors leading into small bedchambers. They passed the rooms quickly and continued to climb.

Soon they reached another landing. It was very dark. Barda moved onto it cautiously. Jasmine, and then Lief, followed.

They could hear the sound of wind whistling around the lighthouse. Straight ahead of them was a red-painted door bearing a large sign.

HALT!

ENTRY FORBIDDEN
TO ALL BUT THE KEEPER
OF THE LIGHT

"The light chamber," Lief muttered. "We cannot go that way."

He and Barda lifted their lanterns high. The flickering light revealed another door, set into the curved stone of the outside wall.

Barda strode to the door, pushed it open, and staggered back as a blast of cold wind hit him in the face. Both of the lanterns blew out. The Kin cried out in panic and pushed forward onto the landing, pressing Lief against the red-painted door.

Lief's skin began to tingle unpleasantly. The wood of the door was warm, and it seemed to be vibrating, as if swarms of bees were crawling on the other side.

The magic of Tora protects me . . .

He tried to push himself away from the door, but he could not move. He felt the Belt of Deltora warming at his waist. And suddenly his mind was filled by a picture of the great amethyst, glowing purple like a great thundercloud pierced by lightning.

I am Adin's heir, he thought suddenly. *I wear the Belt of Deltora. Could that be why fate brought me here? Could it be that I can open the door?*

He put his hand to the doorknob and twisted sharply. The knob turned. Eagerly he pushed. The door . . . began to open!

His cry of triumph was cut short as a hot jolt of pain shot through his hand, his arm, his shoulder. Smoke gushed from the crack in the door, hissing like steam.

Lief's face was burning. He felt as if his hair was crackling. He heard an agonized groan, and realized that the sound had come from him.

The air was filled with hissing smoke. And from the smoke loomed faces, twisted with rage. The face of Red Han — other faces he did not know.

The mouths were gaping wide, shouting. Words were roaring in his ears. "Get out! Get out! Get out!"

Other voices were screaming and calling his name — Jasmine's voice, Ailsa's, Prin's.

He felt himself being pulled away from the door. The searing pain abruptly stopped. But the angry faces were pursuing him, writhing in the smoke.

"They are coming after us!" Ailsa shrieked. "Oh, make haste! Make haste!"

And suddenly cold wind and spray were beating on Lief's face. There was dull light, and the sound of crashing waves. He realized that he had been dragged out onto the viewing platform.

The clouds were boiling and rumbling. The wind was howling. Lightning was cracking the sky.

A door slammed behind him.

"Young fool!" roared Barda's voice.

Lief felt hard hands seize and lift him. Suddenly he was wrapped in warmth, and through his confusion realized that he was in Prin's pouch. He was being rolled and jolted as Prin climbed the railing. The wind was howling like a lost soul.

"It is too wild!" Bruna screamed. "We cannot fly in this!"

"We must!" Ailsa cried. "Oh, they are coming — under the door! Make haste!"

"Go, Prin!" Barda shouted. "Go now!"

Then Lief's stomach lurched as Prin launched herself into the air and was instantly swept away.

5 - The Cruel Sea

Beneath them, the surface of the gray sea heaved like the skin of a vast, angry beast. Above them, dark clouds boiled and tumbled. The Kin struggled against the wind, their great wings beating mightily. But it was hopeless. Every moment the gale was sweeping them farther away from land.

Tossed helplessly in Prin's pouch, Lief watched in bewildered dismay as the slim white shape of the lighthouse grew smaller behind them.

I have caused this, he thought. *It is because I tried to open the light chamber door that we were driven from the lighthouse into the storm.*

But the storm . . . how had it come upon them so quickly?

His heart gave a great thud. Cold certainty settled upon him like a shroud.

The Shadow Lord had found them at Bone Point

and seized his chance. He had summoned up the storm. He had sent the wind racing from beyond the mountains to sweep them away.

Away from the land. Away from Deltora. So that . . .

Horror stabbed Lief as he realized that while his face and hands were icy cold, the Belt around his waist was warming. It was growing hot — hot as fire.

The memory of his father's gentle voice filled his mind.

It is death to take the gems beyond Deltora's borders . . .

Even for me, Lief thought wildly. *Even for Adin's heir. For there is older magic than the Belt of Deltora — older magic than the dream of Adin. The ancient magic that bonds the gems, and the dragons, and the land . . .*

And the Shadow Lord knows it.

The Belt was scorching his flesh. It was as if every one of the gems was a red-hot coal.

Prin could feel it. She had begun to gasp and whimper. Her wings were faltering. And still the wind swept them on, on.

Lief looked down. Surging gray water. White-capped waves.

The tide is coming in . . .

He knew what he had to do. He could not afford to think. He had to act now. Now!

He heaved himself up and over the edge of Prin's pouch. And with her cry of shock ringing in his ears, he plunged down, down, into the sea.

He hit the freezing water and went under. For a

few terrifying moments he sank, blind, deaf, his arms flailing helplessly. Then, his lungs almost bursting, he managed to claw his way up.

As his head broke through the surface a dark shape splashed into the waves beside him. He looked up just in time to see Ailsa, her pouch empty, swept away by the howling wind.

"Barda!" he shouted, and choked on a mouthful of salty water.

Barda's head bobbed up beside him, sleek and dripping. Barda's arm reached for him urgently.

Lief shook his head. "I am all right!" he gasped. "I did not fall. I had to jump. But you — "

"You *jumped*?" Barda bellowed, drawing back his hand and treading water furiously. "Are you mad, boy? Why — ?"

"The Belt . . ." Lief's voice failed him. His body was racked with cold, and at the same time burning with heat. Steam was rising from the icy water around him.

Barda's eyes widened as he understood. Rapidly he looked around him.

"There!" he shouted. "Lief — this way!"

Lief turned in the water. Through the dimness he saw the narrow, pale shape of the lighthouse in the distance and the white froth of waves pounding on the shore. With Barda beside him he struck out, trying not to panic, trying to ride the tide towards the land.

"Jasmine!" he sputtered. "Where — ?"

"We both saw you fall," Barda panted. "Jasmine could do nothing, because she cannot swim. She is still up there somewhere, with the Kin. Worried out of her life, no doubt."

Lief looked up. He could see nothing but racing clouds. The Kin, and Jasmine, had been swept farther out to sea.

They will be safe, he promised himself. *Much safer than if I was with them. The Shadow Lord seems to know my every move, so by now he must know that I jumped into the sea. He will let the wind die, for why would he spend his power to no purpose? Then the Kin will be able to fly back to land.*

The Belt was cooling. He could feel it. He knew that this meant that he had managed to move a little closer to shore.

The relief was intense. But his teeth were chattering. His arms and legs were aching and numbed with cold. More and more often his head slipped below the surface of the surging water.

A wave surged over him. Again he went under. Again he forced his head up to the air, his throat aching. He could no longer see the shore. There was a mist in front of his streaming, stinging eyes.

This cannot go on much longer, he thought grimly. But still he pushed towards the sound of the shore, trying to ignore the aching numbness of his legs and arms. He was determined to get as close to land as he could before cold and exhaustion finally overcame him.

Almost certainly he and Barda would be dead by the time the tide tossed them up on the rocks, or onto the sand of the little bay beside the lighthouse. But the Belt would be found.

He could hear Barda splashing heavily at his shoulder, and his heart smote him.

Barda had watched over him almost all his life. At first he had not even been aware of that steadfast protection. Then he had often resisted and resented it. Lately, he had come to take it for granted that whatever he did, Barda would always be by his side.

But Barda has his own life, Lief thought. *Or at least — he has a right to it.*

A picture of Lindal flashed into his mind — Lindal, standing tall and straight by the gates of Broome, the palms of her hands pressed to Barda's in long, wordless farewell.

Barda could have found happiness, after all the years of struggle, Lief thought. *Instead, he will die with me in this cruel sea.*

"I am sorry, Barda," he choked. "I am so — "

And at that moment, his bare foot kicked against something hard.

Stunned, he turned in the water. And through the mist that filmed his eyes he saw, looming dark above him, the side of a ship.

For an instant he stared, unable to believe his eyes. How could a ship have come upon them so silently? How could he have missed seeing it, even in this strange, misty dimness?

He shouted to Barda, then hailed the ship at the top of his lungs. Barda was soon calling with him. But no light appeared above them, and there was no answering call.

Long oars hung from small dark holes ranged along the ship's side just above the waterline. Gasping, Lief reached for the oar closest to him. But even as his fingers closed on the wet, splintery wood, he knew it would be of little use. The oar was too low to be used as a step to the deck. And the hole it poked through was far too small to admit anything bigger than a rat.

"Keep shouting, Lief!" gasped Barda, moving up beside him. "We must *make* them hear us."

Then Lief felt something brush against his free hand. His fingers closed around thick, wet rope. And as he looked up again he saw with amazed joy a rope ladder trailing over the side of the ship, its base disappearing beneath the foam.

"Barda!" he croaked.

"I see it!" He heard Barda pant behind him. "Go! I am with you!"

Lief seized the ladder in both hands, found a rung with his feet and, gritting his chattering teeth, began hauling himself upwards.

He had climbed only about halfway to the deck before he realized that there was something strange about the ship.

It was riding very low in the water, and instead of tossing from side to side in the swell, as he would have expected, it was gliding as smoothly as a fish. This made his climb easier, but a sense of foreboding was growing within him as he forced his aching body on.

As he neared the top of the ladder he paused, his scalp prickling. He could not rid himself of the feeling that he was being watched. Yet he could see no glimmer of light above him. He could hear no voices. The only sounds were the creaking of the timbers and, now and again, a faint, mouselike squeaking.

He glanced quickly from side to side and noticed, very near to his right shoulder, the remains of some painted words.

The ship's name, Lief thought. *So we must be at the front of the ship — the bow.* He peered at the name, trying to read it.

T E A Y L C

So much of the paint had flaked off that Lief could make no sense of the fragments that remained. Yet somehow he felt that he should have been able to. There was something about the pattern made by those last flakes of paint that was familiar. Something he had seen before . . .

"No captain of a working ship would let its name wear away like that," Barda muttered from below him. "This is a hulk — abandoned. And some years ago, by the look of it."

Lief was certain that Barda was right. The ship was drifting. The eerie squeaking he could hear was the sound of the wheel spinning from side to side on the deserted deck.

But someone — or something — was aboard. He knew it. Something had sensed them. Something was holding its breath, waiting . . .

"Keep moving, Lief," Barda growled. "Whatever is up there, we must either face it or drown. And I would rather die fighting."

So Barda senses danger, too, Lief thought. *At least we are prepared.* But forcing himself to climb the last few rungs of the ladder was one of the hardest things he had ever done. His legs felt as if they were made of stone. His whole body was weighed down by dread.

He reached the top. He saw crawling mist, a tangle of ropes and sails, the wheel swinging slowly, with no hand to guide it. He saw the jagged stub that was all that remained of the ship's main mast.

A moving picture leaped into his mind like a flash of vivid memory. He saw the ship tossing in a ferocious storm. He saw giant waves crashing over the deck. He heard the terrible, screeching sound of the mast snapping in two, and the terrified cries of drowning men.

Visions of the past . . .

He slid over the side of the ship, onto the deck. Shivering and panting, he crawled aside to make room for Barda. As he did, something made him look up. His heart seemed to fly into his throat.

A woman in a long blue robe was standing motionless on the prow of the ship. She was staring out to sea, leaning forward slightly, her hands clasped over her heart. Mist billowed around her, but nothing on her stirred — not a fold of her robe or a curl of her long red hair.

Her face, with its stubborn chin, its steady gray eyes, was strangely familiar.

Lief's mouth went dry as he realized who she was. And as Barda thudded onto the deck beside him, he suddenly realized, too, why the fragments of the ship's name had rung warning bells in his mind.

This abandoned, drifting hulk was Laughing Jack's ship, *The Lady Luck.*

And the woman standing so silent, so motionless on the prow was Red Han's daughter, Verity.

6 – Ghost Ship

Lief and Barda crawled to their feet, dripping and shivering. The deck creaked beneath them. Behind them, the wheel squeaked and spun. The figure of Verity did not stir.

"It is not real, Lief," Barda muttered. "See how it leans over the water, as if to guide the ship? It is a figurehead, carved out of wood and painted. Many ships have them. You must have seen pictures — "

"Yes," whispered Lief, through chattering teeth. "But I have never seen a figurehead that looks as real as this. And it is Verity to the life. I think — "

His voice faltered. It seemed to him that the rigid figure on the prow turned its head very slightly, as if it had heard him. Or had his eyes been deceived by the drifting mist? He clutched the Belt at his waist . . .

Suddenly there was a flurry of movement, glaring light, and a roar of sound. Seabirds shrieked. Water splashed. Harsh voices cheered, shouted, and guffawed.

Then they were no longer alone. A crowd of grinning men jostled all around them.

Cursing in shock, Barda reached for his sword.

Lief did not move. He knew that the men could not see them. This was the crew of *The Lady Luck*, as it had gathered on deck eighteen years ago to enjoy the sort of entertainment it liked best.

Two men were tying a girl to a short pole fixed to the prow. The girl was wearing a long blue cloak.

"Verity," Barda breathed.

The men had placed Verity so that she was facing the lighthouse that gleamed white across the water.

"Ah, what a fine figurehead she makes, to be sure!" jeered a rat-faced man in a striped woollen cap.

"Too scrawny for my taste!" bawled a hulking brute with a black patch over one eye.

"She will be scrawnier yet when the birds have finished with her, Beef," a third roared, baring teeth like crooked yellow pegs.

The whole crew laughed uproariously.

The girl made no sign that she had heard them. She did not struggle as loop after loop of rope wound about her, binding her to the pole.

Laughing Jack was standing beside her, peering through a telescope. He stood as still as a tall, thin statue, his bony shoulders rigid, the sharp line of his jaw intent. After a moment, he lowered the telescope and turned to Verity, the edges of his wide mouth curving into a smile.

And just for an instant, as he turned, he reminded Lief of someone else. *Someone I know*, Lief thought in confusion. *Who . . . ?*

Then the smile broadened into the familiar death's-head grin, and the illusion vanished.

"Your father is watching, girl," Laughing Jack sneered. "He is in the light chamber."

Verity made no answer.

Laughing Jack moved a little closer to her. "Sound carries well across water," he said. "Red Han will hear you if you scream. You would do well to begin now. The sooner he gives in, the sooner you will be free."

"My father will never give in, James Gant," Verity said. "And I will never call to him."

Laughing Jack's eyes narrowed. "Fine words," he hissed. "But they will not last. Soon you will be begging for food and water, beaten to rags by the wind and the waves. And then the hungry birds will come. You will scream loud enough when they begin to feast on you, girl, make no mistake."

He turned on his heel and strode away from her, directly towards Lief and Barda. The crew stumbled out of his way, some falling over in their haste.

Lief and Barda stood their ground. Laughing Jack passed through them like a gust of icy breath. And in that moment, the vision vanished, and they stood blinking on the creaking deck, mist floating all around them and the silent figurehead their only companion.

"If ever I have the chance to lay my hands on

that grinning monster, he will know what fear is," Barda muttered at last.

His eyes were fixed on the figurehead. His fists were clenched.

He is remembering the girl he saw painting on the beach of the little bay, Lief thought. *The happy girl in the yellow skirt that fluttered in the wind.*

"We do not know the end of the story, Barda," he said. "Red Han may have given in after all. Verity may have been returned to him. Then they may have fled Bone Point together."

"I doubt it," Barda muttered.

Lief doubted it, too. His mind was seething with questions, but the vision he and Barda had just seen was proof to him that *The Lady Luck* had been the setting for frightful deeds. The ship was haunted by memories so terrible that they would not die.

With a heavy heart he turned away from the figurehead. Whatever he had suspected before, he was sure now that it was only a carving.

The skin of the figurehead was smooth and undamaged, the steady eyes untouched. And the scavenging birds would not have left them so.

After Verity's wasted, torn, and lifeless body had been at last cut down, Laughing Jack had no doubt enjoyed replacing it with a likeness of her as she had been. What better way to torment the father who had refused to do his will?

Lief shuddered all over and suddenly became

aware of just how cold he was. His teeth had begun chattering again. Water was dripping from his hair and clothing. His feet felt like blocks of ice.

"We must go below deck and try to find a way of warming ourselves," Barda said. "I can see no lifeboat. No doubt it was taken when the ship was abandoned. We will have to stay here until the storm ends and the Kin return for us."

"There is no storm here," Lief murmured.

They both looked up. The mist moved softly all around them. They could see no sky, no sea. They could hear no wind, no thunder. It was as if the world beyond *The Lady Luck* had disappeared.

"We must find a way of warming ourselves," Barda repeated stubbornly. "We must rest and regain our strength. After that, we can think what to do."

Plainly he was determined not to let dread take hold in him. He was fighting it back in the way he knew best — by concentrating on practical things.

And he is right, Lief thought. *If we panic, we will certainly perish.*

Together they stumbled towards the swinging wheel, stepping over tangled ropes and the tattered remains of canvas sails. Not far behind the wheel there was a narrow door set into a raised portion of the deck.

Barda put out his hand to open it, then glanced back at Lief.

Lief pulled aside his coat and looked down at the Belt of Deltora.

The ruby was pale. *Danger*. The emerald was dull. *Evil. A broken vow.*

"Are they sensing the present, or the past?" Barda murmured.

Lief did not know.

He saw that the lapis-lazuli, the heavenly stone, bringer of good fortune, still sparkled with points of light like the night sky. It was strong. If dangers still lurked below deck, at least they would have some protection. And it was cold, so cold . . .

He took a breath and nodded.

Barda opened the door. A breath of sour air escaped into the mist. A short flight of steps led steeply down.

They took the steps cautiously. At the bottom they found themselves in a small square space, facing a door made of richly carved wood.

Above the door was a dusty panel of colored glass, etched with words and symbols:

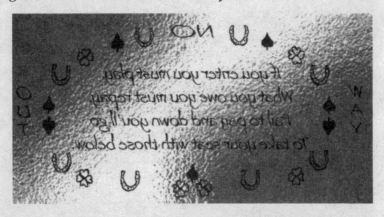

"This is a very fine door for a working ship," Barda murmured. "And it seems to have been a way out, rather than a way in. Well, that does not matter to us."

He peered at the dingy glass panel. "The decorations are all symbols of good fortune. Now why — ?"

Then he slapped the side of his head in annoyance. "Of course! *The Lady Luck!* Now I know where I have heard that name before! I heard a traveller mention it, in my first years of playing the beggar in Del."

He nodded slowly, remembering.

"*The Lady Luck* was a gambling ship — a floating gaming house — that once sailed the River Tor," he said. "It had an evil reputation, though the man I heard tell of it had not seen it for himself. The ship disappeared from the Tor, he said, before the Shadow Lord invaded, and no one knew what had become of it."

"Well, now the mystery is solved," said Lief grimly. "*The Lady Luck* had sailed down the Tor and out to sea. Laughing Jack was following his master's orders. He was on his way to destroy the Bone Point Light."

As he spoke, he was squinting at the small words in the center of the glass panel.

"You cannot read those," Barda said impatiently. "Not in this light, without a mirror. They will only make sense from the other side."

He seized the handle of the door. "Come! The main saloon must be beyond. With luck we will find a stove there. And candles and other supplies, perhaps. Captain James Gant would have made sure his guests had every comfort — while they still had money to lose, in any case!"

Lief hesitated. Something about the carved door made him uneasy.

He looked around and noticed for the first time that another door led off the small space. It was to his left — a thing of plain, flat metal, with a solid lever for a handle.

"Perhaps this leads to the crew's sleeping quarters or the galley," he said. "Let us try it first."

Without waiting for an answer, he pushed down the lever and pulled the metal door open.

Dimness. The sound of water, softly lapping. And a smell so vile that Lief staggered back.

"What is it?" Barda hissed behind him.

Lief was gasping for breath. His eyes were watering, as though the foul air gusting from the space beyond the door was filled with poison.

And at that moment, the mist drifting down the steps brightened, as if softly lit from above.

"The moon is rising," Barda said. "Lief — "

Lief rubbed his eyes and stared into the dimness.

At first he could see only shapes. Then, gradually, he took in the full horror of the scene before him.

He was looking down into the belly of the ship — into the half-submerged cavity where once the rowers had sat, plying their oars.

Where they sat still . . .

Waist-deep in water, half-rotted bodies slumped over the oars. Rusted chains hung like bracelets from their bony wrists. Sea worms coiled around necks and fingers, and snails with speckled shells clustered thickly on the rags that still clung to their bones.

Lief felt the blood drain from his face. He heard Barda cursing softly behind him.

"They were left to die," Barda muttered. "How? Why? What happened here?"

What happened here?

Lief's teeth were chattering. His head was spinning.

He could see . . . he could see a fleshless skull with a black patch still hiding one eye socket. And beside it, a grinning head covered with the dingy, rotted remains of a striped woollen cap.

The soft glow of misty moonlight drifted through the dank, flooded space. Chains clinked softly in the darkness. The slumped horrors seemed to stir . . .

With a cry, Lief staggered back and slammed the door.

"In here!" Barda seized the handle of the carved door and pushed forward. Lief stumbled after him . . .

Into a sudden blaze of light.

7 - Fool's Gold

Stunned, Lief and Barda stood blinking as the door swung softly closed behind them. Whatever they had expected, it was not this.

The long room looked as if it had been deserted only moments before they entered. It was deliciously warm. Thick red carpets covered the floor. A fire crackled in a marble fireplace. Candles burned in sparkling crystal holders hanging from the ceiling. Long, gold-framed mirrors lined the walls, reflecting the room's contents over and over again.

Scattered everywhere were small, polished tables surrounded by comfortable chairs. On some of the tables there were decks of cards. On others there were dice. Still others carried game boards and wheels, games of skill, games of chance. In the center of every table was a gold-edged card explaining the rules of the game, and a tall glass container filled with gold coins.

An open treasure chest brimming with many more gold coins stood to the left of the doorway where Lief and Barda stood. A large notice was fixed to the inside of the open lid.

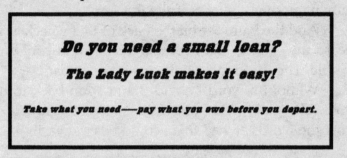

Do you need a small loan?

The Lady Luck makes it easy!

Take what you need—pay what you owe before you depart.

"It is all an illusion," Barda said, edging away from the chest and drawing his sword. "It must be!"

Lief put his hand upon the topaz. He had learned long ago that the great gem had the power to banish illusions. But nothing in the room wavered or changed appearance.

He crouched and tested the carpet with his fingers. It felt soft and warm. As he straightened, he saw that steam had begun to rise from his wet clothes. They were already drying.

"This is no illusion," he said slowly. "It is real. Somehow, it is real!"

"If we keep our wits about us and touch nothing we should be safe," Barda said. "The moment our garments are dry, we will go back on — "

He broke off, his eyes widening in shock. He glanced down at his feet, then rapidly up again.

"What is it?" Lief hissed. But as the words left his lips, he felt it, too.

Something about the ship had changed. It was no longer simply rocking gently in the tide. It was moving, moving purposefully forward.

And the hair rose on the back of Lief's neck as he heard the sounds that even the thick carpet could not muffle. The rhythmic, creaking sounds of oars.

Without a word he and Barda spun back to the door. The glass panel above it seemed to glow. And now the words etched there could be read easily.

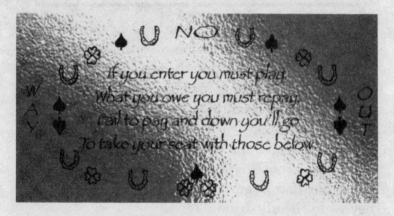

A cold weight seemed to settle in the pit of Lief's stomach. Slowly he looked down.

There was no handle on this side of the door.

Barda snatched his dagger from his belt. He tried to push the point of the dagger into the crack of the door, but the weapon stopped abruptly just short of the carved wood, as if repelled by an invisible barrier.

Barda grunted in surprise and tried again. Still he could not touch the door.

And neither could Lief. For long minutes they both struggled vainly to break through the shield. Whatever they tried, their hands, feet, and weapons bounced back without making contact with the door or the glass panel above it.

"This is useless," Barda panted at last. "The shutting spell is as strong as the barrier that seals the mountains in the Shadowlands."

"Why not?" Lief said bitterly. "The Enemy provided it to *The Lady Luck*, no doubt, in return for Laughing Jack's useful services."

They both looked up at the glass panel. During their vain attack on the door, the ominous message seemed to have grown larger and brighter.

Barda turned his back on it. "If this door is closed to us, we will find another!" he said, and determinedly began to survey the long room.

Lief turned, too, but his heart was heavy. "Barda, I do not think — " he began.

"Just look!" Barda muttered fiercely. "There *must* be another way out. We have only to find it."

The mirrors winked back at them, reflecting chairs and tables, game wheels and boards, coin jars and candles, and their own figures.

But at the far end of the room, directly ahead of

them, there was something that the confusing reflections had disguised at first glance.

It was a painting, the same size as one of the mirrors, and framed in exactly the same way. It was difficult to see clearly, because it gleamed in the light, but it seemed to be a view of land and sea.

"There!" Barda exclaimed. "That painting marks our way out, I am sure of it."

He hurried forward. Putting his doubts aside, Lief followed, dodging through the maze of tables and chairs so as not to touch or disturb anything.

They moved on and on, their boots sinking into the thick carpet. Their reflections walked with them, multiplied over and over again in the mirrors so that it seemed that the grand room was filled with bedraggled wanderers.

"I did not realize the room was quite so long," Barda called over his shoulder. "The mirrors are deceiving."

He began to walk a little more quickly. Lief followed in silence, trying to shield his mind from images of the rotting corpses bending and straightening as they plied the oars. But with every step he became more aware of the relentless sounds of movement below his feet and the faint, unpleasant odor drifting in the warm air.

The minutes dragged by. But their reflections in the mirrors at the end of the room did not grow larger, and the tables ahead never became less.

At last Barda's firm steps faltered, and he stopped. He turned to Lief, his face grim.

"The first line of the rhyme was, 'If you enter, you must play,' " Lief said reluctantly. "I fear that we will not be able to leave until one of us at least plays a game."

Barda clenched his fists. "We cannot play!" he almost shouted. "From what I have seen, the games must be played with gold coins, and we do not have a single one between us!"

For answer, Lief glanced over his shoulder at the treasure chest gaping beside the room's entrance.

"No!" Barda shook his head violently. "We would be mad to fall into that trap, Lief! What if we lose? We will not be able to repay the loan!"

Fail to pay and down you'll go . . .

"We will not lose," said Lief, ignoring the tightness in his chest. "And in any case, we have no choice."

"You have seen for yourself what happens to people who borrow from Laughing Jack, Lief!" exclaimed Barda. "How can you even think of it? Ah, what fools we were not to divide the gnomes' gold between us! It is all with Jasmine, and who knows where she — "

"If you have a better plan than mine, Barda, pray tell me what it is and stop wasting time!" Lief cried furiously.

He did not want to think about what might be

happening to Jasmine. Jasmine, who could not swim. Jasmine, pitching dangerously over the raging sea in the pouch of the smallest and most fearful of the Kin.

He saw Barda eyeing him, and wondered if his companion guessed the reason for his anger.

With a muttered apology he turned away and began hurrying around the polished tables, searching for a game he thought he could win.

It was soon clear that most of the games depended far more on luck than skill. Despite the lapis-lazuli glowing on the Belt, Lief did not wish to trust his and Barda's safety to chance. Yet every game of skill he saw cost two or even three gold coins to play while promising only small winnings, while the games of chance cost only one coin, and success paid well.

"Laughing Jack encouraged his guests to trust their luck rather than their brains," he murmured.

"Of course," Barda said sourly behind him. "That way, he had far more chance of stripping them of everything they had — and more."

Trying to ignore the chill running down his spine, Lief went on looking.

At last he came to a small table at which there was only one chair. On the table, as well as the coin jar and the printed card, was a gold cloth about the size of a handkerchief. The cloth was plainly covering something, but it was impossible to tell what it was.

There were only a few words on the card.

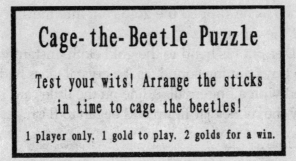

Cage-the-Beetle Puzzle

Test your wits! Arrange the sticks
in time to cage the beetles!

1 player only. 1 gold to play. 2 golds for a win.

"This will do," Lief said. "We have solved puzzles like this before."

Very aware of Barda's eyes burning into his back, he strode to the treasure chest and took a single gold coin. As he was turning away, he found to his surprise that several more coins were sticking to his fingertips.

For a moment he was tempted to keep them, in case he needed to play more than once. Then he realized that he was being lured into borrowing more than he had intended. He turned abruptly and brushed the extra coins back into the chest.

Clutching his one gold piece, he quickly moved back to the table.

"I do not like this," Barda growled. "There is a time limit, Lief. That is clear from the notice. And it is Jasmine who is good at this sort of game."

"Jasmine is not here," Lief snapped. "We are. And surely between us we can see the answer. Especially with the topaz to aid us."

He sat down. Barda stood close behind him and

watched as he slipped the gold coin into the slot at the top of the money jar.

Lief put his hand to the gold cloth. Instantly there was a tiny chiming sound, as if a crystal glass had been tapped with a fingernail. A line on the little card standing by the money jar lit up and began to flash.

1 player only . . . 1 player only . . . 1 player only . . .

Lief's stomach seemed to turn over. He wet his lips. "You will have to move away, Barda," he said. "It seems I must play the game alone."

With a muttered curse, Barda moved back. The words on the card continued to flash. Barda moved away, farther, farther . . .

And suddenly the words on the card grew still and the gold cloth vanished.

"I can see nothing from here," Lief heard Barda call in a low voice. "I cannot help you."

Lief did not answer. He was concentrating fiercely on the objects revealed on the tabletop.

Thirteen silver sticks had been arranged to make six rectangles. Inside each rectangle was a little jewelled beetle. Below the pattern was a small piece of parchment:

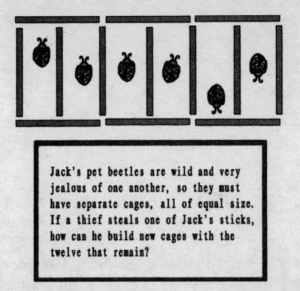

Jack's pet beetles are wild and very jealous of one another, so they must have separate cages, all of equal size. If a thief steals one of Jack's sticks, how can he build new cages with the twelve that remain?

As Barda had feared, a small glass timer stood beside the puzzle. Lief glanced at it and saw that fine sand had already begun trickling through the narrow tube that linked the timer's two chambers.

When the top chamber was empty, his time would be up. The timer was the same size as the one used in the forge kitchen for boiling eggs, so he knew that he had less than three minutes to solve the puzzle.

Three minutes to win back what he had borrowed.

Three minutes . . .

Beneath his feet oars creaked and chains rattled.

Fail to pay and down you'll go
To take your seat with those below.

8 - Truth

His heart thudding painfully, Lief picked up one of the silver sticks and put it aside. Now twelve sticks remained on the table, and one beetle's "cage" had only three walls.

With his left hand on the topaz, he hunched forward and with his free hand began moving sticks around, desperately trying to find the solution. But whatever he tried, he could not make six cages of the same size.

What you owe you must repay . . .

The sand was running, running. The top chamber of the timer was already half empty.

Calm your mind, Lief told himself. There is a trick here. A trick! You must relax enough to see it!

He moved his fingers from the topaz to the amethyst — the amethyst that calmed and soothed.

Peace stole through him. His racing mind slowed. And as it did, a thought occurred to him.

If the puzzle was to make cages with twelve sticks, why had there been thirteen sticks in the first place? And why had the sticks been arranged as they were?

To throw me off the scent, he guessed suddenly. *To fix my mind on cages of a certain shape . . .*

He looked at the silver sticks with new eyes. And then he saw the answer.

He glanced at the timer. Only a tiny pile of sand remained in the top chamber. He had just moments left.

Swiftly he rearranged the sticks and put the jewelled beetles in place.

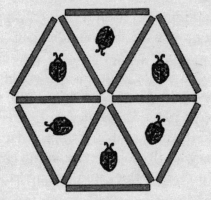

The last grain of sand slipped through the timer. Silently a slot opened at the bottom of the money jar and two gold coins slipped out. Lief snatched them up with a cry of triumph and leaped from the chair.

Barda groaned with relief. Lief swung around to face him, holding up the coins in his closed fist.

"Two coins!" he crowed. "One coin to pay our debt, and one to keep for a souvenir!"

"A souvenir!" Barda called, shakily wiping sweat from his brow. "By the heavens, I could well do without a souvenir of the last few minutes. I believe they took ten years off my life!"

Lief's excitement abruptly died. For a moment, the thrill of winning had made him forget where he was. Now he remembered only too well.

The cursed beings below his feet were still rowing. The sounds chilled his blood. Every stroke of the oars was pulling the ship farther away from Bone Point, further away from hope of rescue.

"Let us get out of this prison," he muttered.

Quickly, keeping close together, he and Barda walked back to the treasure chest.

"We have played a game, and hereby we repay our debt," Lief said loudly. He threw one of the coins he had won onto the golden pile in the chest.

They turned and began to move towards the far end of the room.

This time they made progress, and in moments they were standing before the painting — staring at it in astonishment.

The picture was smooth as glass, but within it a painted sea moved sluggishly and clouds drifted in a red-stained sky.

And rising in the center, unmistakable, was the tall white shape of the Bone Point Light.

Barda drew breath sharply. "What is this? It seems alive! It moves, like a reflection in a mirror. But it is a painting! Only a painting of the Bone Point Light as seen from — "

"From the sea," Lief finished. His scalp was crawling. "I think this *is* a mirror, Barda. Or it *was*. Look at the signature. Verity made this image. It is her view of the Bone Point Light from the prow of *The Lady Luck*."

He rubbed his sweating hands on his coat. "Verity was a prisoner, but no ordinary one, it seems," he said. "Somehow she made an image of what she could see appear in this mirror. She did it with the power of her mind, just as once she used paint and paper to make the pictures hanging on the lighthouse walls."

"It cannot be!" Barda shook his head in disbelief.

"Verity was born in the lighthouse," Lief said quietly. "Toran magic filled the air she breathed from her earliest days. It would not be surprising if she had powerful gifts of her own — though even she may not have been aware of it until . . ."

"Until wickedness and terror came into her life for the first time, in the person of Captain James Gant," Barda finished heavily. "Then, it seems, her gifts woke.

Not soon enough to save her, but in time to leave this image behind, in memory of all she had lost."

Lief nodded, then frowned. Suddenly he was imagining what practical Jasmine would say to that.

"But why?" Jasmine would exclaim. "If Verity could not use her magic to save herself, why did she not spend it on some useful purpose?"

Some useful purpose . . .

Lief looked again at the painting. And this time he saw something that he had not noticed before.

"Barda," he said slowly. "Did you know that the name 'Verity' means 'truth'?"

"Yes," Barda said. "What of it?" Unwilling to abandon his hope that the painting concealed a hidden door, he was running his fingers around the gold frame, vainly searching for a spring or catch.

"There are things in this painting that are not true," Lief murmured. "Do you see?"

Barda paused, glancing at the image. Then he frowned and stepped back a little, to see more clearly.

"For one thing, the viewing platform is missing from the lighthouse," Lief said.

He stretched out his hand and touched the place where the viewing platform should have been. Instantly his fingertip tingled and beneath it something glowed.

Barda gasped, and Lief snatched his hand away. He rubbed his hot fingertip, staring at the painting in amazement.

Where his finger had been, the viewing platform now glowed brightly, its red railings vivid against the whiteness of the tower. And — was it his imagination, or was the Light above a little stronger?

I will shine like truth through the darkness . . .

"The little bay, where I saw Verity first, is missing also," Barda said slowly. "It should be there, on the left — the north side — of the Point. But the painting shows only rocks."

Lief nodded. Again he put out his hand and touched the place. And again, instantly, the painting changed. The Light brightened further, and beneath his fingertip, where only rocks had been before, the little bay glowed, complete with seaweed, shells, and a smashed red boat.

"But the boat was surely not broken in those days!" Barda exclaimed. "Verity used it for fishing!"

"No doubt Laughing Jack wrecked it before he took Verity back to the ship," Lief said. "To prevent Red Han from rowing after them when finally he escaped from the locked room."

As he spoke, he noticed that the sounds below their feet had grown louder, and the movement of the ship less smooth. It was as if the dead rowers were becoming restless.

"The water," Barda said huskily. "It is too still. The waves are not foaming on the rocks. And look! The birds are carrying stems of water berries.

People on the coast use them for food and drink. But seabirds do not. They are — flesh-eaters."

He hunched his shoulders and rubbed the back of his hand over his mouth, as if he wished his last words had remained unspoken.

Lief stretched out both hands. He touched the water at the end of the point, and the berries carried by one of the birds.

He felt a jolt, and jumped back with a sharp cry. This time, with the touch of his fingers, the whole painting had changed.

An entirely different scene was now within the frame. It was the deck of *The Lady Luck* — and it was not a painting. It was real.

Lief felt Barda's hand close on his wrist. Perhaps Barda was speaking, but he could not hear him. His ears were filled with other voices, the calls of birds, and the creaking of ship's timbers.

Figures were moving beneath the smooth surface of the glass — the rat-faced man in the knitted cap, the man with the black eye-patch, and all the rest of the ship's motley crew.

A loop of rope drooped from the rat-faced man's hand. The brute with the black eye-patch was holding a sword. Both were sweating, wild-eyed, and spattered with blood. The rest of the crew were sullen, shuffling, their eyes fixed on the silent figure tied to the pole at the ship's prow.

Verity had plainly been suffering for many days. Her hair hung over her shoulders in a limp, tangled mat. Her cloak and nightgown were stiff with salt. Birds were flying about her head in a swirling cloud.

. . . the hungry birds will come. You will scream loud enough when they begin to feast on you, girl . . .

Lief wanted to turn away, but he could not. The moving image held him fast. And a voice, whispering in his mind.

Look! See! This is the truth of it! The truth . . .

Beyond the cloud of birds, far over the smooth blue water, the Bone Point Light burned defiantly. Red Han had not given in.

The flock of birds parted slightly. Lief's heart thudded as he saw Verity's face clearly for the first time. To his astonishment, it was smooth and unmarked. And as he watched, a bird carrying a tiny branch of water berries moved very close to the girl's mouth and hovered.

Verity opened her lips. The bird pressed the berries into her mouth and held the branch steady as she ate.

They are feeding her! Lief thought dazedly. *Instead of attacking her they are —*

His heart gave a lurch as a harsh voice cried out angrily. He watched, transfixed, as the crew stumbled aside and Laughing Jack strode onto the deck, his teeth bared in fury.

"Did I not tell you to drive the birds away from

her, Scrawn?" Laughing Jack snarled to the rat-faced man with the rope.

The man called Scrawn cowered. "I have been trying, Captain, on my honor," he whined. "My arms fair ache with trying."

He jerked his head at the man in the eye-patch. "Beef tried, too, with me, and a dozen others in turn. But those birds are crafty, Captain. While we fight off one lot, more are sneaking in to her beneath their wings."

"It's not natural," grunted Beef. "The creatures are bewitched."

"And the sea is cursed," called someone from the back of the crowd. "There's been not a wave or a breath of wind since the girl came on board."

"It is true!" The man with the crooked yellow teeth was gnawing his thumb nervously. "Seven long days, and still the witch lives, watered and fed by her creatures. Still the Light burns. And here we rot, with the sails hanging limp as rags, and no slaves below to row us — "

"Silence!" thundered Laughing Jack. His hollow eyes blazed as he stared at Verity, the fluttering birds, and, beyond them, the Bone Point Light.

9 - Mutiny

Abruptly the moving picture vanished and Lief and Barda found themselves staring once more at Verity's painting. The pastel image drifted slowly below the surface of the glass, mysterious and full of secrets.

But it will give up its secrets to those seeking the truth, Lief thought. *That is why it is here. We must correct the lies. Reveal what is hidden . . .*

Slowly he became aware of a rising chorus of groans and mutterings mingling with the creaking of the oars beneath his feet. He glanced around him and saw that the light in the great room had dimmed. The candles were burning low.

"How much time has passed since we entered this room?" he whispered. "It does not seem so long . . ."

Barda moved uneasily beside him. "Come away,

Lief," he said. "Whatever this painting is, or how it was created, we should delve into it no further. Through it, the past lives again. The wretched beings below feel it. And they do not like it."

"If that is so, it is because the truth will set us free," Lief murmured.

"No!" hissed Barda. "What is past cannot be undone and is best forgotten. We would be fools to rouse the rowers further, Lief. Soon the candles will go out, and who knows what will happen then?"

Impatiently he shook Lief's arm. "Come away and help me search for the way out," he said. "We have paid our debt, and according to the rhyme at the entrance, we are free to leave. We have only to find the door."

But Lief did not move. "I would rather trust Verity than Laughing Jack," he said quietly.

His eyes were still fixed on the painting. The Light was brighter than it had been before. The little bay and the viewing platform of the lighthouse still glowed in their places. The painting was now more correct than it had been. But there was more to be done.

A fish was flying among the birds in the air. Lief touched it. It disappeared, then reappeared, glowing, under the water where it belonged. He saw that one of the birds was missing a wing, and that there was a second sun in the sky. He touched both errors, and instantly both were corrected.

Eagerly he turned and scanned the great room. But no new door or gap had magically appeared among the mirrors.

What was more, the room had grown even dimmer. The stink of decay was stronger. And the muffled howls of pain and rage from below, the angry clanking and stamping, were louder.

"Lief!" Barda urged, tugging at his arm.

Lief gritted his teeth. "I must finish this," he said. "I must!"

Barda groaned in a fever of impatience. "The rocks at the foot of the lighthouse are smooth, instead of jagged, as they should be," he said rapidly.

Lief touched the rocks. The change was made. Six corrected errors now glowed on the painting. The Light was shining so brightly that it dazzled his eyes.

But when he looked around, nothing had changed.

"There must be another error to find," he muttered.

Desperately he searched the painting. But he could see nothing more that was wrong. Nothing . . .

Then his eye fell on the bird flying alone, high in the sky, at the far right of the image.

The bird was too large — far too large to be real. He stretched out his hand, and touched it.

And at once the painting was replaced by another moving scene — the noisy, crowded deck of *The Lady Luck*, lit by weird red light. The whole crew seemed to be assembled there. Scrawn, the rat-faced man in the striped cap, was among them. So was Beef, with the black eye-patch, and the man with the crooked teeth.

Verity was still tied to the prow, and the exhaustion on her face made it plain that more days had passed. Across the flat sea, the Bone Point Light was still burning. But the men were not looking at Verity or the Light. Instead, they were all looking up, pointing at the vast bird hovering high above the sea to the south.

The giant bird was not an error, then, Lief thought dazedly. *It was not a painted lie, but truth. Like the flat, calm sea, and the birds with the water berries. But what — ?*

His stomach knotted as he realized what the hovering bird was.

"Ak-Baba!" cried Scrawn. His lips were drawn back from his teeth in a snarl of terror. "And here we lie, like chickens waiting to be swooped on by a hawk!"

"What is it doing?" another man wailed. "Why does it circle over the western sea? What business did it have at the Maze of the Beast?"

Lief's heart thudded. He heard Barda grunt with shock.

"For that matter, why is the sky scarlet, so long after dawn?" grunted Beef. "And those clouds to the east — I will knock down the first man who tells me they are natural."

"Omens!" wailed the man with crooked teeth. "Omens of doom!"

He tore his eyes from the hovering Ak-Baba and fixed them on Verity. She was staring straight ahead, staring at the Light.

"We are cursed!" the man shrieked. "Thirteen days we have lingered here, and still the girl lives. The whole of nature is taking revenge on us for her sake! Our only hope is to free her. Cut her down!"

He took out a knife and started for the prow.

"Stop!" The voice was like the crack of a whip. The man with the crooked teeth froze, and the others shrank back as Laughing Jack strode onto the deck.

"I have had news," he barked. "Unexpected, but welcome. It seems that we are no longer needed here."

He moved closer to Verity. "Your sacrifice has been in vain, witch!" he spat. "Here is something that you and your idiot father did not count upon. The magic that fed the Bone Point Light has died."

"You lie," the girl whispered.

Laughing Jack's skull-like face split in a humorless grin.

"At dawn this day the Belt of Deltora was broken," he sneered. "The seven gems were scattered. The Ak-Baba you now see in the sky carried but one of them. Like the others, that gem will never be found."

Lief felt a shiver run down his spine. He realized

that he and Barda were witnessing events that had happened the very day of the Shadow Lord's invasion — a time before he was born, when so many lives were changed forever.

His eyes were drawn to the lowering clouds on the eastern horizon. Often he had been told of the darkness that swept over Del with the coming of the Shadow Lord. Now he was seeing it for himself.

He glanced down at the seven jewels shining in their medallions of steel as if to remind himself that Laughing Jack was wrong — the gems *had* been found.

Once lost in the Maze of the Beast, the ghastly domain of the Glus, the amethyst, symbol of truth, now shone on the Belt, bright as a great purple star, fiery as the Bone Point Light.

Verity's voice, husky with pain and disuse, broke through his thoughts. Quickly he looked again at the moving image in the golden frame.

"Del may fall, James Gant," the girl said. "The whole kingdom may fall to the Enemy who is your master. But the magic of Tora is ancient. It does not depend on the Belt. By the will of the Torans, the Light will continue to shine."

Laughing Jack's grin broadened. "Indeed?" he said with relish. "Well, here is something you do not know. At dawn the king and queen fled from Del. They asked help from Tora, but Tora broke its vow of loyalty and refused refuge. As a result the Torans have been swept away, exiled by their own ancestors' magic."

Verity's exhausted face seemed to grow a little paler.

Gleefully Laughing Jack rubbed his hands. "You did not expect that, did you, witch?" he crowed. "And you know what it means, I see. The Light burns now only by the will and efforts of your stubborn father. But unprotected he will be easy prey."

"You touch the Light at your peril, James Gant," Verity breathed.

The man scowled. "The Light is no longer my concern," he spat. "It will die of its own accord once your father is gone, and others will see to him. We are to return to the River Tor."

He turned to the gaping crew. "Man the oars!" he snapped. "We must be away with all speed. I have been warned — "

A high sound split the air. Laughing Jack spun around, his eyes wide with shock. Verity was laughing!

"You cannot deceive me!" she cried. "Your master is displeased with you. You failed him! If the Light dies at last, it will not be because of you, but because the Torans broke their ancient vow. *That* is why he denies you the satisfaction of taking your revenge on my father."

"Silence!" Laughing Jack shrieked.

Flecks of foam had gathered at the corners of his mouth. His eyes were wild.

He snatched his knife from his belt and pointed it at the helpless girl.

"You will pay!" he hissed. "You will pay in pain and blood for every day you have defied me. When we are under way — "

He glanced over his shoulder at his men, as if just realizing that they had not moved.

"Why do you stand gaping there?" he shouted. "I gave you an order!"

The men looked at one another. Scrawn licked his lips, then spoke.

"We are not paid to row, Captain," he said sullenly. "*We* did not choose to sail in haste from the head of the Tor to the sea. We begged you to stop along the way — to replace the slaves delivered to the Gray Guards with new ones to man the oars. But you would not listen."

Lief felt a thrill of horror. So the final fate of the unlucky gamblers who borrowed from Laughing Jack had been even more terrible than he had imagined. They had manned the oars of his ship for a time, certainly. But they had ended their lives as slaves in the Shadowlands.

"How dare you question my orders!" Laughing Jack barked. "The ship is becalmed, you fool! If we are to move, you must row. Get below!"

Beef slowly shook his massive head. "Too many

have died down there, Captain," he grunted. "It is unwholesome."

Laughing Jack bared his teeth in fury. "We — must — get — to — the — Tor!" he hissed. "Or at least, for now, away from this cursed Point, with its rocks and shallows, to a safe harbor farther south."

When the men still did not move, he stabbed a bony finger at the eastern horizon.

"A great storm is coming!" he almost screamed. "Do you not see it?"

"We see it, right enough," called the man with crooked teeth. "And whoever summoned it — the red-headed witch now tied to the prow or the sorcerer you call your master — we will never outrun it."

He turned to the rest of the crew. "I say this ship is finished! This ship, and its captain, too."

"Mutiny!" shouted Laughing Jack. "You will hang for this, Coffin!"

The man called Coffin made no sign that he had heard.

"We owe James Gant no loyalty," he roared. "You all know what he is! He supplies slaves to the Shadowlands, and in return he has this ship, fine food and drink, and some of the sorcerer's powers he craves. But is this all he has? Oh, no!"

He bared his peglike teeth. "With my own eyes I have seen his treasure chest in the gaming room. It overflows with the gold he cheats from his victims before sending them to the oars. But has he ever offered to share this bounty with us? No! He has become as rich as a king, while we toil for a pittance!"

"So why should we risk our lives for him?" grunted Beef.

"Indeed!" Coffin shouted. "I say we take the lifeboat and make for the shore — take the girl with us and release her. Perhaps then the sea's vengeance will fall where it deserves — on our brave captain! Let him use his magic to save himself — if he can!"

10 - Deadly Bargain

Most of the men roared agreement. Those nearest to Laughing Jack drew their swords and daggers. His face twitching horribly with fear and anger, Laughing Jack took a step back.

"Wait!" he cried, his voice cracking. "Wait! I will make a bargain with you."

The men hesitated.

"Do not listen to him!" shouted Coffin. "He lies as easily as he breathes!"

"No! Hear me!" shrieked Laughing Jack, clasping his hands. "I have treated you unfairly — I see that now. But I will make it up to you, if only you will help me."

Coffin scowled and shook his head. The other men looked uncertainly at one another, then at the storm clouds rushing towards them from the east.

"Beware!" cried Verity. "Whatever you swear here will bind you. I cannot prevent it."

"What is your offer, Gant?" Scrawn snapped, ignoring her.

"I do not want to lose my ship!" quavered Laughing Jack. "*The Lady Luck* is all that is important to me. So I promise you this: all the treasure will be yours to share if you will man the oars until others are found to replace you!"

He cast his eyes down humbly, but Lief saw that he was peeping at the men beneath his eyelashes, and that his thin mouth twitched at the corners as their faces brightened with greed.

Scrawn wiped his mouth with the back of his hand.

"How do we know you will keep to your bargain, Captain?" he asked gruffly. "How do we know that once the ship is safe you will not break your word?"

Laughing Jack looked up and solemnly placed his hand on his heart.

"All the gold is yours, my loyal crew," he said in a trembling voice. "If I take one piece of it for my own, I myself will take to the oars. I swear it on my soul!"

"I hear your words, James Gant, and they will bind you!" cried Verity from the prow, her voice as shrill as a seabird's call.

Laughing Jack's eyes widened for an instant, then he sneered.

"So!" he said. "According to the witch, my oath cannot be broken. Now, what of you, men? Do not fear, your time at the oars will not be long. Your replacements will soon be found."

He grinned evilly. "You know that the gaming room is a web. You know that human flies blunder into it gladly, and often. And you know that never, unless I will it, do they struggle free. Sooner or later the fools borrow, then cannot repay their debt."

"That is because for every coin they borrow they must pay back three, Captain," sniggered Scrawn. "But that lying sign on the treasure chest says no such thing."

Lief's stomach turned over. He heard Barda give a low groan.

"Why, Scrawn, my little sign does not lie!" said Laughing Jack, raising his eyebrows in mock innocence. "It says plainly, 'Take what you need — pay what you owe before you depart.' It is not *my* fault if my guests mistake its meaning, and assume that the two sums are the same."

The crew laughed uproariously.

"You twist the truth for gain, James Gant!" Verity called. "You use the powers granted to you to revel in lies and wickedness. But I will set my mark upon this ship. I may die, but the truth will live for those who wish to see it, and the truth will set them free."

Laughing Jack's grin did not falter. He paid no more attention to Verity's words than to the shrieks of the swooping birds. His eyes were fixed on his men, willing them to listen only to him.

"So!" he said heartily. "Do we have a bargain?"

The men were grinning, nodding, rubbing their hands. Plainly they were convinced — dazzled by the promise of riches beyond their wildest dreams.

"No!" screamed Coffin. "You fools! You will doom us all!"

Beef's lip curled. His dagger hand jerked forward.

With a low groan, Coffin crumpled and fell lifeless to the deck, blood oozing from the deep wound in his back.

"Very well, Captain," Scrawn said softly, as Beef wiped his blade clean on his jacket. "We will take the places of the slaves until others are found to replace us. Agreed, mates?"

"Agreed!" the men around him bellowed.

"I hear your words, crewmen, and they will bind you!" cried Verity.

And in the blink of an eye, Laughing Jack stood alone on the deck with the captive girl and the sprawled body of Coffin, while from below came the hideous sounds of sliding chains and men shrieking in terror.

Laughing Jack stood dumbfounded, his wide mouth gaping.

Look! See! This is the truth of it! The truth . . .

"Your men are at their oars, James Gant," whispered Verity. "They have taken the places of the slaves indeed, and the chains the slaves bore are their chains now. They are bound by their oath, as you are bound by yours. I warned — "

Her voice broke off in a choking gasp. With a hiss of rage, Laughing Jack had spun around and stabbed her to the heart.

Lief heard himself cry out in horror. Through a scarlet mist he watched as Laughing Jack pulled his dripping knife free.

Seabirds wheeled and screamed above the dying girl's head as her life's blood drained away, flowing down, down over her white nightdress, over her bare feet, down to the sea.

And as the first gleaming red drops touched the water, the sea heaved as though in anguish.

Cool, foaming water sprayed on Verity's twisted body. The healing, loving tide flowed over her. And when it fell back all that remained on the prow was a wooden figurehead, its hands clasped to its breast.

With a roar, huge waves rose and crashed onto the deck of *The Lady Luck*, knocking Laughing Jack from his feet, tumbling him over and over in swirling foam. Coffin's dead body tumbled with him, battered and beaten against the deck.

More waves rose, and more, pounding down as if the sea was a mighty beast trying to tear the ship to pieces. Awash with foaming water, the ship rocked violently, tipping first to one side, then the other. With a groaning shriek the tall mast snapped and crashed to the deck.

Below, the chained men screamed in terror, screamed for release as water poured into their prison and engulfed them. But Laughing Jack paid no attention to them. He did not even glance at the door that led to the rowing bay.

Intent only on his own survival, he was crawling to the lifeboat, tumbling into it, sawing with his knife at the ropes that held the boat above the water.

"Master, save me!" he babbled. "Master, I beg you . . ."

Red-rimmed clouds swept in from the east. The sound of the storm mingled with the crashing of the waves. And in the midst of the storm, a voice spoke, hissing like meat on a spit:

"You are a fool, slave. You deserve to perish. But I still have need of you . . ."

There was a flash of brilliant light and a terrifying clap of thunder. Lief and Barda staggered back, clutching each other, deafened and half-blinded.

And when they looked again, the golden frame was filled once more with the painted view of the Bone Point Light.

The six errors Lief had corrected were glowing still, and the Light was shining like a star. When they turned to look at the rest of the room, however, all they saw was darkness. The candles had died at last.

They stood, motionless, calming themselves,

vainly trying to make out the shapes of tables, chairs, the carved door, and the treasure chest at the other end of the room. But all they could see was the painting behind them, and the small patch of red carpet at their feet. It was as if they were on a tiny island in the midst of a coal-black sea.

"Our time has run out, it seems," Barda muttered.

It was then that Lief became aware that the groans and cries from below had ceased. They had been replaced by a tense, waiting silence that was even more terrifying.

For a moment the silence held. Then Lief stiffened. A stealthy, sliding, brushing sound was coming from somewhere ahead, at floor level.

"What is that?" he hissed. He jumped as he heard the sound again, this time from somewhere to his right.

Suddenly there were brushing, sliding sounds by the dozen, coming from every direction. There were gusts of freezing air, thick with a smell so vile that he could hardly breathe.

And there was the drone of muttering voices.

"Beware!" Barda exclaimed, jerking Lief back.

Only then did Lief see his danger. A square section of the scarlet floor directly in front of him was sliding away, sliding slowly aside with that same faint brushing sound, revealing a yawning pit of inky darkness.

The stench of decay and stagnant water rose from the pit. And, in the darkness, things moved. The painting's soft glow fell first on the mottled tips of grasping, ruined fingers, then on arm bones, reaching, clad in tatters and clinking with chains. Below were the ghastly, upturned faces of dead rowers, hollow eyes burning, grinning mouths muttering, muttering . . .

"My replacement . . . mine, mine . . ."

Lief shrank back as the grasping fingers felt around the edge of the pit, close, so close to his feet that he imagined he could feel the cold breathing from the scraps of flesh that still clung to the bones.

He did not dare speak. His ears were filled with the sound of his frantically beating heart.

He longed to run from the evil-smelling pit, the seeking, clawing hands. But looking out into the darkness, he knew that traps like the one before them must riddle the floor of the room.

He and Barda could not move. One false step and they would be lost.

He touched the Belt of Deltora. The topaz, the gem of faith. The lapis-lazuli, the heavenly stone. The amethyst, for peace and truth.

Faith. Truth . . .

Verity's words seemed to ring in his ears.

I may die, but the truth will live for those who wish to see it, and the truth will set them free.

Slowly, carefully, Lief turned to face the painting.

Without comment, Barda turned, too. Barda knew now that this was their one hope.

They were so close to the wall that their faces were almost touching the image. It was hard to see it. But . . .

Seven errors. Seven . . . there must be . . .

"The road!" Barda whispered suddenly. "The road to the lighthouse is missing! It was neglected and overgrown when we saw it, but surely in the time of Red Han it was — "

"Of course!" Lief pressed his finger on the place where the road should have wound from the hills.

His fingertip grew hot. The painting seemed to shimmer as the road appeared, a snaking, glowing ribbon leading away to the distant hills. And the Light . . . the Light was suddenly blazing like a beacon.

I will shine like Truth through the darkness . . .

Lief spun around. The Light pierced the dark. Its broad, brilliant beam made a bright path over the red carpet, lighting up the black squares that squirmed with grasping fingers. The path led directly to the sealed, carved door.

And the door was opening!

Howls rose from below.

"Run!" Barda roared.

Together they ran along the path of light, dodging the pits filled with claws reaching up to seize their ankles. They reached the doorway and hurtled through it, pounding up onto the deck.

The angry cries of the cheated rowers floated after them. The deck trembled beneath their feet as unseen hands beat it from below. At the prow, just visible through the mist, the figurehead that had been Verity stared forward gravely, hands pressed to its heart.

Both heard the soft voice in their minds at the same time.

Flee this place. Trust the clean sea.

And without hesitation both of them ran to the side of the ship and leaped overboard — plunging recklessly into the cold, dark water.

11 – In the Dunes

Afterwards, Lief and Barda remembered nothing of their time in the sea but that desperate leap, and the black water closing over their heads. When they regained their senses, they were lying on a golden shore in a tumble of shells and seaweed.

They could see by the sky that it was early dawn. Dimly they could hear waves rolling in, regular as a great heartbeat. But where they lay, all was still. The sea had cast them up in the night and left them to sleep.

Stiffly they sat up, staring around them, then at each other. They could not believe that they were alive.

The shore stretched away on either side of them, marked only by the shells and weed of the tide line and the sticklike tracks of birds. Before them was the open sea. Behind them were sand dunes, rising one behind the other as though mimicking the waves.

"We have been swept south, I think," Barda said after a moment, his voice rough with salt. "Far south of Bone Point — beyond the Maze of the Beast, beyond the mouth of the Tor. How could this be?"

"Before we leaped into the sea, the ship was moving," Lief rasped in reply. "It was moving for quite a time. It . . ."

He scrambled unsteadily to his feet. Now that he was fully awake, he was aware of an uneasy, prickling feeling — like a warning of danger. Perhaps he had felt it even as he slept, he thought. He seemed to remember the scraps of dreams, urging him to wake.

He scanned the sea, but saw no sign of *The Lady Luck*. He looked left and right. The shore was deserted. He turned towards the silent dunes. And at once the uneasy feeling grew stronger.

But it was not warning him away from the dunes. It was calling him towards them. Calling him . . .

Quickly he glanced down and even in the half-light saw red and green gleams in the Belt at his waist. The ruby and the emerald were undimmed. They sensed no danger.

And the call was urgent.

"We must go," he muttered. Without even waiting to make sure that Barda was following, he almost ran to the base of the first dune, and began to climb.

The dry sand slipped beneath his feet with a squeaking sound as he struggled upwards. By the time he reached the top of the dune, his legs were shaking.

There was nothing ahead of him but another hill of sand, even higher. He ran awkwardly down the first dune and began climbing the second, again not stopping till he reached the top.

Bewildered, he stared ahead.

Dunes, nothing but sand dunes — pink, mauve, deepening to purple, rising against the brightening sky. There was no sign of movement anywhere. But the call was even stronger.

A wave of dizziness swept over him. His knees buckled and he half fell, half stumbled down the side of the dune, tumbling at last into a heap at the bottom.

He lay there, his head swimming. Sand showered over his legs as Barda slipped down after him. Then he felt a hand lift his head and a water flask was pressed to his lips.

He drank gratefully, then opened his eyes. Barda was crouched beside him, replacing the flask's cap.

"Tell me what you are doing, Lief, and I will follow you more willingly," Barda said wearily. "These dunes remind me unpleasantly of the Shifting Sands. Who knows what lurks within them?"

"I am sorry," Lief muttered, pushing himself up so that he could prop his back against the base of the third dune. "I . . . I felt a call. Very strong. I thought of — Jasmine."

Barda shook his head. "Jasmine could not be here. The wind that swept the Kin away from the lighthouse was blowing west, not south. If Jasmine and the Kin survived the storm, they would have returned to Bone Point, to search for us there."

"*If* they survived," Lief repeated dully. He turned his head away to stare sightlessly along the shadowed cleft that lay between the dunes.

Barda's own heart was very heavy, but doggedly he pressed on.

"We can do nothing for Jasmine. Our task is to take care of ourselves now," he urged. "This call you feel — it may be a trap. The Shadow Lord . . ."

His voice trailed off as he saw that Lief was no longer listening. Lief's eyes had widened. His mouth had dropped open.

Into the sudden silence came the soft sound of falling sand. Barda's scalp prickled. He put his hand to his sword and slowly turned to follow Lief's eyes.

Something was rising from the shadows of the cleft — a huge and terrible head, swaying on a twisting, gray-scaled neck that was still half-buried in the third dune. The beast's fangs were bared in a silent snarl. Its eyes opened — dull, flat dragon eyes.

"Do not move." Barda heard Lief breathe, his voice almost as soft as the whisper of the falling sand.

The dragon's head swayed. Sand showered from its murky scales and poured from between the sagging spines around its snarling jaws.

"Come closer, king of Deltora," it rasped.

Lief climbed to his feet, his face haggard with shock.

"No, Lief!" Barda whispered. "Keep back! This is no real dragon, but a copy, like the false, twisted beast at Dragon's Nest! Its color is proof of it."

Without speaking, Lief looked down at the Belt of Deltora. Following his eyes, Barda saw first the bright gleams of the ruby and the emerald. But then, just before Lief's hand closed over it, he saw that the great amethyst, gem of truth, was flaming like purple fire.

Astounded, he watched as Lief moved forward, one hand on the amethyst, one hand outstretched.

The dragon's eyes seemed to widen as Lief drew closer. Slowly its neck bent, until its head was resting on the sand.

And as Lief's outstretched hand touched the cold, gray ridge of bone above its eyes, the eyes closed, and the dragon gave a great, shuddering sigh.

"You have almost been the death of me, king," it murmured. "Often, in my suffering, I have cursed you in my mind, I confess it. But you have come at last. Now I can only hope that you are not too late."

❄

Hours passed before the dragon spoke again. Lief remained by its side, his hand upon its brow.

Slowly, as the amethyst worked its magic, the dull gray of the dragon's scales changed to mauve, then to purple. Slowly the spines beside its jaws stiffened and its snarling jaws relaxed. Every now and then it struggled, as if trying to free itself. But still only its head and part of its neck were visible above the sand.

At last its eyes opened. Lief saw that they were no longer dull, but gleaming like pale violets.

"You are better," he said.

The dragon snorted faintly. "I am better than I was," it said. "But that is not saying a great deal. Now I know what it is to be as weak as prey. It is not enjoyable."

"No, it is not," Lief agreed.

He hesitated, then decided to take a risk.

"What happened to you?" he asked abruptly. "How did you come to be so near death when we found you?"

"HOW?" thundered the dragon, lifting its head. Lief and Barda shrank back. The dragon coughed, and lowered its head to the sand again.

"I felt you in my land," it said. "I felt the amethyst call me, from far away. It was just as Dragonfriend had said it would be. My oath to him swam into my dreams, and I awoke in my hiding place beneath the sand."

The scales on its head and neck seemed to quiver.

"But the dune had grown since first I buried myself within it," it went on. "The sand was heavy and I was weak with hunger. I began to struggle upwards — then, suddenly, you were gone and I was left stranded, without the strength to free myself."

Its eyes burned reproachfully.

"Just after we crossed your border, we were swept out to sea, through no fault of our own," Lief said.

"It was the Shadow Lord's doing," Barda put in fiercely, as the dragon gave a low growl. "We nearly died ourselves as a result of it, dragon. And it is as well you know it!"

The dragon barely glanced at him. "Dragonfriend said that I would wake at your coming," it said to Lief. "He did not say I might die in the attempt."

"Dragonfriend — Doran — believed, I think, that if the Belt of Deltora was worn constantly by Adin's heir once more, this would mean that the Shadow Lord had been destroyed," Lief said reluctantly. "But, sadly, this is not so. Deltora is free, and the seven Ak-Baba no longer patrol our skies. But the Shadow Lord is still powerful. Even in exile, he tries to destroy us."

"Ah!" The dragon nodded its great head. "Yes. And — I seem to remember that I thought this would be so. I seem to remember telling Dragonfriend that the Enemy would never give in."

Its mouth twitched. "But, of course, Dragonfriend would not listen. Dragonfriend was fiery and impatient. He was intent upon his plan, and did not want to hear objections."

"He wanted to save you," Lief said quietly, then recoiled as the beast's eyes flashed.

"Do not think you have to make excuses for Dragonfriend to me, young king!" the dragon hissed. "Dragonfriend was the best of his kind! He had the heart of a dragon, and he was my true friend. But only fools refuse to see the faults in those they love."

Lief swallowed and nodded, feeling young and clumsy.

Slowly the spark of anger faded from the dragon's eyes.

"Dragonfriend is dead, no doubt," it said, after a moment. "If he was alive, he would have come with you, to find me. And the weight of sand I feel upon me tells me that many years have passed since we said our farewells."

"Yes," Lief said awkwardly. "I am sorry."

"Ah." The dragon grew very still. "And are his bones shut up in some grim place of honor in a human city? Or do they lie beneath a mossy stone in a wild place, as he always hoped they would?"

Lief hesitated. He saw Barda open his mouth to speak, and shot him a warning look.

The dragon was weak and grieving. Now was not the time to add to its burdens. He did not want it to know that Doran had not been honored, but had been thought mad by all his people at the last. He did not want it to know that its friend had died in a frantic, doomed search for proof of the Four Sisters — and died, horribly, no doubt, at the Shadow Lord's hands.

The upstart has the fate he deserves . . .

Lief's stomach churned at the memory of that cold voice hissing from the dying crystal on the forge in Del.

"We do not know where Doran lies," he said at last. "He never returned from — from his last adventure."

The dragon nodded without surprise. "Then, in a way, his wish was granted," it said.

It tilted its head and looked at the sky. "It is strange to think of a world without Dragonfriend in it. Strange and lonely, for after the last of my tribe was gone, he was the only friend of my heart."

Sighing, it lowered its head on the sand once more. "But I will see him very soon, and hear his laughter, where my ancestors fly above the wind," it murmured. "He will be with them, I am sure, for he always said that dragons were more his kin than those of his own kind."

"But — but what do you mean?" Lief exclaimed.

The dragon looked at him with what seemed to be surprise. "I am dying," it said simply. "Do you not understand? You came too late, king of Deltora. Even the amethyst cannot help me now, it seems. I thought perhaps . . . but it is no good. My time of struggle was too long. I cannot find the strength to free myself, and so my place of refuge will become my tomb."

"Do not say that!" Lief cried.

"Why?" the dragon asked. "It is the truth."

"But you have been imprisoned only for a single night, dragon!" said Barda, in the tone he might use to encourage exhausted troops. "Surely you are not so feeble!"

The dragon's eyes slid in his direction for the briefest of moments, then moved back to Lief. "Your friend's ordeal in the sea has addled his brains," it said. "Does he — ?"

Abruptly it broke off. It lifted its head, and its forked tongue flickered in and out, tasting the air.

"Arm yourself, king!" it muttered. "We are invaded."

12 - Surprises

Lief and Barda crawled up the side of the dune and peered cautiously over the top. They were staring straight into the sun, but they could see, shimmering in the distance, a long, wavering shape.

The shape was approaching fast — very fast. Its center was dark, but at each end, bright colors flapped like wings.

Then Lief's dazzled eyes suddenly made sense of what they were seeing. The shape separated into five separate shapes — five figures, hand in hand.

The figures at each end wore long, flowing robes — one scarlet, one blue. Of the others, one was tall and dark, another a small blur of blue-gray, and the one in the middle . . .

Lief stared in disbelief. His heart gave a great thud. The next moment, he was scrambling to his feet, shouting, waving both arms wildly above his head.

Barda was roaring and waving beside him, but Lief was hardly aware of it. Dizzy with joy, he had eyes only for the black-haired girl in the center of the shimmering line, and ears only for her thin, distant cries floating to him over the sand.

A black bird became visible, soaring above the girl's head.

Kree, Lief thought dazedly. *Kree, flying . . . but — but he is only just keeping up with them! How . . . ?*

And then he realized that the robed figures were Zeean and Marilen of Tora, and understood. He himself had sped on the wings of Toran magic.

He watched, fascinated, as the five swept towards them.

※

Long would Lief remember that reunion in the place he learned to call the Sleeping Dunes.

First there was Jasmine, scolding, laughing, and crying by turns as she embraced him. Then there was Josef's former assistant, Ranesh, beaming, with his arm around Marilen, pumping his hand. And Zeean, her wrinkled face made young by joy. And Manus of Raladin, small hands clasped and button eyes wide, as speechless as he had been when first they met him, but this time with relief.

After that came a series of shocks.

There was Lief's and Barda's shock on learning that *The Lady Luck* had been invisible to all who searched for them, and that they had been missing not for a single night, but for ten long days!

There was the shock of the newcomers when, filled with awe, they gazed upon the dragon of the amethyst imprisoned in the dune.

There was the dragon's shock when Zeean briskly insisted that it was not going to die. And its even greater shock when, not long afterwards, a hundred Torans swept into the Dunes, raised their arms, and sent the sand that imprisoned it flying, freeing it at last.

"I did not expect this," the beast told Zeean, flexing its mighty limbs and gingerly unfolding its crumpled, sand-crusted wings. "I had accepted my fate. But I thank you, woman of Tora."

Stiffly, it bowed.

Zeean bowed also. "To assist you was our privilege, dragon of the amethyst," she said. "Long may you fly Toran skies, and your descendants also."

"We will see," said the dragon. And raised its wings to the sun.

✳

There was so much to talk about, so much to explain, so many questions to be answered.

"Ten days!" muttered Barda. "How can it be?"

"Time stands still on *The Lady Luck*, it seems," Lief said.

He glanced out to sea and for a moment thought he caught a glimpse of a dark, ragged shape and the moving sticks of oars.

He stiffened, looked again, and saw only white-

110

flecked water and the purple sheen of the dragon slowly wading in the shallows.

His heart thudding violently, he turned back to his companions. Clearly they had noticed nothing.

"I arrived in Tora to inspect the Bone Point Light," Manus was exclaiming. "Little did I know that I would be searching for lost friends instead!"

The ship was my imagination, Lief told himself. *It was a shadow — a vision born of fear. That is all.*

"It has been a dark time," Zeean sighed. "The morning after Jasmine and the Kin called for our aid, we in Tora felt a shadow pass, as though a cloud had swept over the sun. I thought this was a sign that you were no more."

"I did not believe it," Jasmine said stoutly.

"You did not," agreed Zeean, smiling. She looked apologetically at Lief and Barda. "By the end, Jasmine was the only one of us who still had hope that you would be found alive. The rest of us were certain that we were searching only for your drowned bodies — and the Belt."

Lief gripped Jasmine's hand as Zeean told the story.

Every day Jasmine had joined the search. Every night she had drunk Dreaming Water and fixed her mind on Lief. And after nine nights of emptiness, suddenly there Lief was — alive! — lying on a shore with Barda, in a place where dunes rose like waves running back from the sea.

"When Jasmine woke me and told me of the place she had seen, I knew it was the Sleeping Dunes," Zeean said. "We came at once — but I confess I had little hope. How could you be so far south, almost at the border of our territory, and yet still live? I thought Jasmine's dream was one of wishing, rather than of truth. How glad I am that I was wrong!"

✳

At sunset, Toran tents fluttered like giant silken butterflies on the dunes. A great fire burned brightly, and the smell of cooking mingled with the tang of the sea. The amethyst dragon, refreshed and fed, had removed itself to a quiet place farther down the shore.

Lief, Barda, and Jasmine, sternly bidden by Zeean to rest, sat together under a purple silk canopy a little away from the others. It was growing colder, but none of them wanted to move.

They had resisted Zeean's efforts to persuade them to return to Tora for rest. The evil chance that had delayed them had also brought them very close to their goal. They wanted to press ahead with all speed.

It had been more difficult to resist Ranesh's urgent desire to go with them.

"Whatever you are doing, wherever you are going, I can surely be of use to you!" Ranesh had argued as soon as he had been able to speak to them alone.

"You are already being of use," Barda said. "Are you not helping to rebuild Where Waters Meet, the town of your childhood?"

Ranesh's eyes darkened and he turned his head away.

"That work is complete," he muttered. "The people who have returned have safe homes — for all the good it does them, since food is scarce, the well is sour, and the waters of the Tor and the Broad are not fit to drink. I am spending most of my time in Tora now. And Tora — though it is Marilen's home — is not really to my taste."

Lief could well imagine it. Ranesh's love for Marilen had taken him to Tora, but clearly the quiet, elegant life of the magic city did not suit him.

Any more than it would suit me, Lief thought. *Ranesh must loathe the fact that none of the luxuries Tora provides can be used for the people starving outside its walls. The food of his father-in-law's table must be dust and ashes in his mouth.*

Ranesh's mouth twisted in a rueful smile.

"Also, Josef can reach me all too easily in Tora," he said. "Almost every day a messenger bird arrives with a letter from him complaining about Paff's mistakes and begging me to return to Del. But how can I return?"

He shook his head in despair. "I do not know that I even *want* to spend the rest of my life working in a library! And even if I did, I cannot leave Marilen! Yet how can I keep refusing Josef, when I owe him so much, and he is in such trouble? I feel I am in a trap!"

He frowned as if he felt he had revealed too

much. Then, without saying anything more, he strode away across the Dunes.

"I pity him greatly," Jasmine said. "I know what it is to feel useless — and trapped. I felt the same in Del, while I still lived in the palace, and before I began training the messenger birds. It was a kind of torture."

"Ranesh has spent too long living on his wits to settle into a life where everything is made easy by magic," Barda agreed. "But we cannot take him with us. He must solve his own problems, as best he can."

Silence fell. Jasmine began feeding Filli some nuts she had found in her pocket. Barda drew out the puzzle box he had carried with him all the way from the Os-Mine Hills.

Lief watched him idly. Two smooth rods now protruded from the carved surface of the little cube, but the box remained stubbornly locked. He wondered if Barda would ever discover its secret.

He leaned back, and paper crackled under his cloak. With a start he remembered the little wax-sealed packet Zeean had discreetly passed to him.

"Messages for you from Del, sent before knowledge of your disappearance reached anyone there," she had whispered.

Wearily, he took the packet out, and lifted the wax seal with his thumbnail.

Three small papers were inside, folded closely together. He unfolded them almost with dread. He knew that no news from Del could be good.

LIEF,

I rejoice to hear that all is well with you. Thank you for sending the curious sample of plant life, which I found most interesting.

Rumours abound in Del about your travels and whereabouts. No doubt news of your latest adventures will reach eager ears very soon, and cause even greater interest. I hope this does not inconvenience you too greatly.

I know what a bore it is to find a safe means of sending messages while you are travelling, so will not expect to hear from you for a time. I expect Sharn soon, and will tell her all your news.

My greetings to Barda and Jasmine.

DOOM

PS. I enclose a note from Josef, who for weeks has been wild to contact you. He is missing you and Ranesh greatly, and is in frail health. But I find it hard to be patient with him, I fear.

The first paper was covered in writing he knew well.

Lief shook his head ruefully. He realized that Barda and Jasmine were looking at him and passed them the note.

"Not in code?" Barda said in surprise, glancing at the letter.

"There was no time to work in code, I imagine," said Lief. "Doom expected us to stay in Tora only for a few hours, and wanted to be sure his message reached us. But the note *is* in code of a sort."

Jasmine had been reading her father's note carefully.

"So it is!" she exclaimed. "His real meaning lies under the plain words. He rejoices that the Sister of the North has been destroyed. He recognizes the piece of Boolong cone, so knows we sent our message from Dread Mountain. He warns us that the Shadow Lord will now be even more intent on stopping us — "

"As if we are not all too aware of that!" snorted Barda.

"And he tells us not to write again too soon," said Lief. "Plainly his fear that any message will fall into the wrong hands is even greater than it was before. Only the sentences about poor Josef, added at the end, are what they seem."

He turned to Josef's letter — two pages hastily torn from a little notebook.

He smiled. How Josef must have hated being forced to send such a rough message! It would have offended all his ideas of what was proper. Quickly he scanned the first page of the note.

Your Majesty,

My mind is all confusion.
I have just heard that I may at last
send a note to you if I make haste.
I wish I had been given more notice,
but I must not complain.
Since you left, I have put aside work
on my new book. Instead I have been
studying certain important maps and
writings in the <u>Deltora Annals</u>, hoping
to assist you in planning the next
stages of your journey. The results of
my study have shocked me more than
I can say.
If I am right, the danger is very great.
I fear for you, and for us all.

Lief frowned. He turned to the second page, which proved to be even more confused than the first.

I pray that I am in error, but only you can tell me if I am. Doom refuses to say where you are going. Perhaps, as he claims, he does not know. He has grown very moody of late. I fear he does not trust me. I hope he will not suppress this letter because I have spoken too plainly.

Please reply urgently. Quite apart from the perils outlined above, something about my results worries me, but as yet I have not been able to put my finger on what it is. If only I could clear my mind—

I must finish. Doom is in the hallway, calling angrily for my note.

In haste—

Josef

"What does the old windbag say?" Barda yawned.

"He says that Doom is moody, and that we are in danger," Lief said dryly.

Jasmine laughed. "Well, that is news indeed!" she said. "Does he say nothing else?"

Lief sighed again. "He thinks that by studying Doran's maps and writings he has worked out where we are going. He wants me to tell him if he is right."

Barda looked up. "You will not do so, I presume?"

"Of course not." Lief lay back, frowning, and closed his eyes. He did not like to think of Josef waiting vainly for an answer to his urgent request.

And there was something else. Lief's frown deepened. He had ignored the fussy old librarian before — and regretted it. Josef's mind was sharp, and he knew the *Deltora Annals* like no one else.

. . . something about my results worries me . . .

"Lief!"

Lief's eyes flew open. Manus was standing in front of him, his small face screwed into an apologetic smile.

"I am sorry to disturb you, Lief," Manus said softly. "But I have a promise to keep."

He held out a small package wrapped in white paper and tied with string.

"On my way to Tora from Raladin, I stopped at Tom's shop to buy a packet of No Bakes for the journey," he said. "Tom gave me this. He said it was for you."

13 - Strange Tidings

Lief stared at Manus in astonishment and growing dismay. How had Tom, the strange shopkeeper of the Plains, guessed where he was? They had told no one but Doom that they planned to visit Tora. Even the Kin had not known where they were going until they were in the air.

Yet the wind came to Bone Point, Lief reminded himself. *The wind from the Shadowlands, which swept us out to sea and nearly killed us all. The Shadow Lord knew where to find us. And now, it seems, Tom the shopkeeper . . .*

"Did you tell Tom you would see me in Tora, Manus?" he asked sharply.

Manus's eyes widened. "Of course not. How could I?" he squeaked. "I did not know it myself! I thought you were still travelling in the north-east, and so I told Tom. In fact, I told him he should keep the package, for you would very likely visit his shop yourself, before too long."

"And what did Tom say to that?" Barda demanded.

Manus wrinkled his nose. "He just smiled, in that knowing way he has, and said I might see you when I least expected it. He said I was to give you the package with his compliments, but no one else was to know of it."

He saw the companions glance at one another and his face grew troubled.

"It seems you are not pleased," he murmured. "I hope I have not done wrong."

"No, no, Manus!" Lief said quickly. "We are only surprised, that is all."

He took the package and turned it over in his hands. There was nothing written upon it at all.

"Open it, Lief!" Jasmine urged.

Lief pulled off the string. The wrapping paper fell away to reveal a jar of fire-making beads and a bag of large, round, pink-striped sweets that smelled strongly of peppermint.

"There!" exclaimed Manus, leaning forward. "He has sent you a gift!"

"A gift from Tom?" snorted Barda. "I do not believe it. That man cares only for business. He has never given away anything in his life without being forced into it!"

"There is no note?" Jasmine asked curiously.

Lief shook his head. He smoothed out the thick, white wrapping paper and peered at it in the fading light. Both sides were smooth and unmarked.

Manus glanced over his shoulder at the fire. "The Torans think I am fetching my flute," he murmured. "They would like some music, they say."

"And so would we," said Barda heartily. "Be off, then!"

Manus grinned and scurried away.

The three companions looked at one another, and then at the bag of pink-striped sweets sitting before them on the sand.

"They look and smell very good," Lief said longingly. "But I daresay we would be foolish to eat them."

"Indeed!" Barda said. "It would be best to bury them, or throw them in the fire."

"What reason would Tom have to poison us?" Jasmine exclaimed. "He is a rascal, perhaps, but surely not a villain. He guessed where we were in Deltora, but this does not make him our enemy. After all, Josef claims to have discovered our whereabouts, too, and we do not suspect *Josef* of evil intentions."

"Josef says Doom does not trust him." Lief was frowning. It had been a great shock to discover that their movements were known to so many, despite all their care.

Jasmine snorted. "Doom does not trust anyone but himself," she said.

The sweet sound of Manus's flute drifted to their ears on the cool wind.

Jasmine picked up the jar of fire beads and rattled it thoughtfully. "We know what these are, at least," she said. "They could be very useful to us in the time to come. I will try one now, as a test."

She scraped a shallow hole in the sand before her, then broke the seal on the jar and took one bead. She placed the bead in the hole.

"Move back," she said. "Just in case . . ."

Lief and Barda edged farther under the canopy.

Sitting well back on her heels, Jasmine reached forward and hit the bead sharply with the hilt of her dagger.

The bead burst into flames. Nothing else happened. After a few moments, Jasmine added another bead and soon they were all enjoying the warmth and light of a small but cheery fire.

Barda held his hands out to the blaze and shook his head. "So it *was* just a simple gift," he muttered. "A welcome one, too. But it is very strange."

Lief bent to move the bag of sweets and the discarded wrapping paper away from the fire. As he did, he saw something that made his jaw drop.

Words were appearing in the center of the paper. Dark brown words that had not been there before.

He snatched the paper up. It was stiff and warm.

"Tom sent a message after all!" he gasped. "A

message written in ink that is invisible until it is warmed."

Barda stared at the paper, fascinated. "That was why he sent the fire beads, no doubt — to make sure we lit a fire at once!"

Valued customers—

As you know, Tom does not take sides. He does not interest himself in things that are not his affair.

Due to circumstances beyond his control, however, it seems that your present doings are more Tom's affair than he might wish. Perhaps it was always fated to come to this. Here is some good advice: Should you come across a shop owned by a woman named Ava, do not pass it by. Ava is a vain, cranky creature, but she sees more than most, and can tell you many things of use, if she is willing. She also has boats for hire.

Ava has always adored Peppermint Fancies. The bag enclosed will sweeten her temper and persuade her to help you.

It has been a pleasure to serve you.

TOM

*Note—1 jar Fire Beads: 1 gold coin. 1 bag Peppermint Fancies: 2 silver coins. Please settle this account at your earliest convenience.

**Note—Ava is, by the way, Tom's sister. He would prefer you mention this to no-one else. He has his reputation to consider.

***Note—Burn this.

Lief raised his head from the message, and met his companions' astonished eyes.

Jasmine was the first to recover.

"I am astounded!" she said. "And most of all, I think, to learn that Tom has a sister! It is impossible to imagine him as a child, and part of a family."

"Plainly he *was* a child once, however," growled Barda. "And it sounds as if his sister is as strange a bird as he is."

"Even stranger, perhaps," Lief muttered. "But who is to say we will ever meet her? Her shop could be anywhere."

Still, he carefully tucked the bag of Peppermint Fancies away inside his jacket. He felt excited and uneasy, both at the same time.

Something about the note nagged at him. It was not just Tom's knowledge that they were in the west. It was something else — something he felt he should see, but which eluded him.

Slowly he crumpled the paper and tossed it into the fire. It flared up. One line showed bright in the flames.

Perhaps it was always fated to come to this . . .

Then the paper blackened and crumbled to ash.

✳

The next morning, soon after dawn, the companions left the Sleeping Dunes. They left alone, yet not alone, for the thoughts of the Torans went with them, and sped them on their way.

Barda was the only one of the three who had not experienced the rush of Toran magic before. For a long time he could only stare, wide-eyed, as first the Dunes, then the broad coast road that lay beyond them, slipped rapidly away beneath his flying feet.

At last, he managed to speak. "This is incredible!" he muttered huskily. "Why — in minutes we have gone half a day's march! If only this magic could be harnessed — used all over Deltora. Think what it would mean!"

"The Torans have tried," Jasmine said. "Or so Marilen tells me. But beyond the borders of their territory, their power weakens, then dies. Only between Del and Tora is the path strong, because it was opened by the ancients."

Filli was peeping from beneath her collar, chittering cheekily at Kree, who was flying close beside them. Kree squawked loudly.

"Do not be jealous, Kree," Jasmine grinned. "Soon you will be flying ahead of us again, as is proper."

Sure enough, it was not long before their speed slowed. They were still travelling far faster than normal walking pace, but their surroundings no longer flashed by in a blur. Now they could see pounding waves on their right, and the occasional ruined house amid the barren land to their left.

"You see? We have crossed the border," Jasmine told Barda, as Kree drew ahead of them with a triumphant screech. "The magic is fading."

And we are in the land of the diamond, Lief thought. He glanced down at the Belt of Deltora. The great diamond winked in the sunlight.

He put his hands to the gem, closed his eyes, and willed the diamond dragon to wake and come to him. But he felt no special warmth, no answering glow.

In his mind he saw Doran's Dragon Territories map, and the broad, empty spread of the land of the diamond.

By the time we reach the Isle of the Dead, the diamond dragon will have sensed the Belt, he told himself. *Wherever it lies, however far away, it will wake and come to me, as the other dragons have done.*

It will come if it can, a voice in his mind replied. And Lief's thoughts flew back to the amethyst dragon, as it had been when he bid it farewell at dawn.

"So you are taking the amethyst away, though I am still too weak to fly," the great beast had said.

Lief had swallowed. "I am sorry," he had said stiffly.

"There is no point in grieving over what cannot be helped," the dragon had replied. "Now I am a little stronger, I feel the poison in my land. Its evil source is south of here — beyond my border. The dragon of the diamond must help you defeat it. Is that not so?"

Lief still remembered the wave of relief that had flowed through him when he heard those words, spoken so calmly, and with such dignity.

"I pray that the dragon of strength and purity will

aid you as it should," the amethyst dragon had continued. "But if it should fail you, call me to your side. If it
is within my power, I will come. I will do it for love of
Dragonfriend. I know he would have wished it."

"Thank you, dragon of the amethyst," Lief had
managed to say. He had been very moved.

"And if you call me, king of Deltora," the dragon
had finished, "it would be best, to make sure I hear
you, that you call me by my true name. It is . . . Veritas."

The last words were spoken softly, so softly that
Lief had been forced to bend to hear them. He had
straightened, very aware of the honor he had received.

"I thank you, Veritas," he said humbly. "I swear
that never will I use your name unwisely, and that I
will honor it. My true name is Lief."

The dragon had nodded, but said nothing more.
And quietly, Lief had left it where it crouched, motionless on the sand.

"Look! Ahead! Lief, *look*!"

Lief's eyes flew open at the sound of Jasmine's
voice. He blinked. His heart pounded.

They had rounded a bend in the road, and suddenly the end of their journey was in sight. Suddenly,
they could see ocean not only to their right but to their
left, and far ahead as well.

Before them stretched a long, narrow point of
land. Like a thin flat finger tipped with rock and
fringed with foam it jabbed through the blue of the sea,
stretching away into the distance stretching to . . .

Lief's eyes dazzled. Something was flashing at the end of the point — flashing like the Bone Point Light in Verity's painting.

"What is it?" Barda exclaimed. "Can it be another lighthouse? I thought — "

Kree screeched wildly overhead.

"It is the island!" cried Jasmine.

And as Lief ran forward, squinting, he saw with wonder that it was so. The source of the dazzling light rose from the sea beyond the tip of the point.

High, steep, and bare, the Isle of the Dead shone like glass. Every surface glittered and flashed in the sun, as if the Isle itself was one vast diamond.

In front of the great mass of light, separated from it by a strip of boiling foam, was a small gleam of scarlet.

The first island, Lief thought. *The smaller one shown on the map. It shines like a ruby, just as the other is like a diamond.*

And then, as his eyes moved on to the mainland, he saw something else that the brilliant light of the Isle of the Dead had caused him to miss at first glance.

A gleaming shape was floating above the ground at the tip of the rocky point, burning like a silver beacon against the blueness of sea and sky:

14 ~ Ava

Lief squinted at the gleaming shape. Almost instantly he realized that it was not some strange vision floating in midair, but a huge metal sign. The sign was attached to the roof of a small building that was so brown, low, and rounded that it looked as if it had grown out of the rock.

Ava's shop, he thought, his hand moving to the bag of Peppermint Fancies in his jacket pocket.

He knew he should be amazed to find Ava's shop — any shop — here, in this wild and lonely place.

Yet he was not amazed. And slowly he admitted to himself what in his heart he had known all along.

Tom would not have sent that message and the gift for Ava unless he had been sure that Lief, Barda, and Jasmine would pass this way. He had been certain that the companions' goal was the Isle of the Dead. He knew his sister could help them.

. . . she sees more than most, and can tell you many things of use. . . . She also has boats for hire . . .

Their eyes narrowed against the bright light of the island, the companions moved forward, barely noticing that their feet were now on the ground and that they were moving at normal walking pace.

The point narrowed more and more. At last they reached a place where the road curved to return to the main line of the coast. Ahead was a ragged arrow of rock pointing to the two islands.

Ava's dwelling, topped by its glaring sign, was perched almost at the tip of the arrow. The companions left the road and began to trudge towards the building, their heads bent against the wind.

"A very strange place for a shop," said Barda, shading his eyes as he scanned the rock and the sea beyond.

"It is likely that this place was not so deserted, once," Lief said. "The coast road is very broad — and why would anyone make such a road, if there was no one to travel on it?"

"Besides, Ava's sign is like Tom's," Jasmine pointed out. "It can be read the same way from both sides, so it can be seen from the sea as well as from the road. She may have had customers who came to her in ships."

"If she did, she has them no longer," Barda said gruffly. "There are no ships in these seas now."

Lief glanced at him. There had been an odd tone in his voice.

Barda had turned away from the ocean and was frowning down at his feet. A muscle twitched beside his mouth, and his fists were clenched.

Lief felt a sudden chill. He looked quickly out to sea. But there was nothing to be seen. The only dark spot on the white-flecked surface was a flabby mat of seaweed floating near the shining Isle.

If Barda had seen something else — a ship with a broken mast and slowly dipping oars, for example — it was no longer visible.

Or it was not there at all, Lief told himself firmly. *It is natural that memories of* The Lady Luck *should haunt us. But we must not fall into the trap of believing that the ghost ship is truly dogging our footsteps. That way lies madness.*

Sea spray was cold on his face. The waves seemed very loud. He looked ahead and with a slight start saw that they had nearly reached the end of the point.

Across the sea, the scarlet island glimmered and the high, shining peak of the Isle of the Dead flashed in the sun. And now Lief could see that the two islands were linked by a ragged bridge of rock — a natural arch spanning churning white water.

But closer, much closer, was the glaring sign. Ava's shop was directly ahead.

Brown and hunched, built of rounded stones

mottled with sea moss, the building was larger than it had appeared from a distance.

The front looked like a modest cottage, with a central door and shuttered windows. The back was higher, with bare, windowless walls.

The boat shed, Lief thought. Again his hand crept to his jacket pocket, as if the bag of Peppermint Fancies hidden there was a talisman.

If the diamond dragon answered his call, it might carry him and his companions directly to the Isle of the Dead. But they could not depend upon it. The dragon might not come at all. Or it might come, but be unwilling to carry them. They needed a boat.

Slowly the companions approached the shop. Its low roof was thatched with dried seaweed. Wind whistled about its walls, rattled the shutters that covered its windows, and tore the smoke rising from its chimney into tatters of swirling gray.

A small notice was fixed to the door.

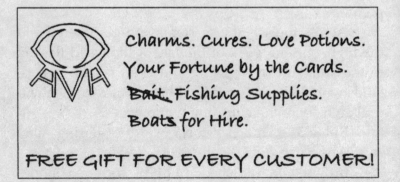

Charms. Cures. Love Potions.
Your Fortune by the Cards.
~~Bait.~~ Fishing Supplies.
Boats for Hire.

FREE GIFT FOR EVERY CUSTOMER!

"Ava is a witch!" hissed Jasmine.

"More likely just a fraud who is as crafty in business as her brother," muttered Barda. He pointed to the last line of the notice. "As I recall, *Tom* promises a free gift for every customer also."

"He does," Lief whispered. "But he only gives it if you remember to ask. I wonder if his sister is the same?"

"Enter, friends, if you are of good will!"

They all jumped violently as the husky voice called from within the shop. With a nervous glance at his companions, Lief pushed the door open.

Inside it was warm and very dim, for the only light came from a glowing fire. The air was heavy with the scents of herbs and smoke.

Peering through the gloom, Lief noticed first that the walls of the room they had entered were lined with shelves that stretched from floor to ceiling. Every shelf was crammed with jars, bottles, tins, and boxes.

Then he saw, crouched in a sagging chair beside the fire, a figure shrouded in a hooded cloak made entirely of the black and white feathers of seabirds.

"You have found Ava," the figure whispered. "What is your wish?"

Lief took a breath, but could not speak.

"A love potion?" Ava muttered. "No. I can see there is no need for that. A cure, then? No . . . not yet a while." She tittered unpleasantly.

Barda cleared his throat. "We would like to

hire a boat, if you please, good lady," he said loudly.

Ava raised her head.

Lief's heart jolted. The face framed by the hood of the feathered cloak was powdered chalky white, even to the thin lips. Dull brown hair hung limply about the hollow cheeks. The eyes were covered by a tightly wound band of black silk.

Then, for the first time, Lief noticed the white stick leaning on one arm of the chair.

Ava, whose symbol was the eye, was blind!

. . . she sees more than most . . .

"I have no boats for hire," Ava said softly.

"The sign on your door says you do!" Jasmine exclaimed.

The woman shrugged. "I have only one boat now," she said. "I do not care to lend it to strangers."

Her thin white lips curved slightly at the corners. For a fleeting moment Lief saw an eerie resemblance to Tom.

"Your brother told us of you, Ava," he said quickly, before Barda or Jasmine could say anything more.

"Brother?" The figure in the chair grew very still.

"Your brother Tom is — a friend of ours," Lief said, feeling in his pocket for the Peppermint Fancies. "He told us that you could help us — if you were willing. He sent you a gift."

Cautiously he moved towards the chair, holding

out the bag of sweets. Ava seemed to have relaxed a little. Her nose twitched, but she did not stir.

Lief placed the gift in her lap and stepped smartly back. He held his breath as hands warm in thick black woollen gloves crept from beneath the feathered cloak and clasped the bag firmly.

"Peppermint Fancies," the woman sighed. "Ah, Tom always remembers his little sister's favorite. Clever Tom! But then, he was always the cleverest of us all, even in the old days. Or so it was said."

She tilted her head slightly.

"It is not like Tom to admit our relationship," she said. "Tom values his privacy, as do I. He must have a special reason for helping you. What might that be, I wonder?"

Again her lips curved into that slightly mocking smile. Again Lief felt a stab of recognition.

But this time . . . this time it was different. This time the smile reminded him not only of Tom the shopkeeper, but of someone else as well.

He caught his breath as memories flooded through him.

It is a matter of business . . .

Due to circumstances beyond his control . . . your present doings are more Tom's affair than he might wish. . . . Perhaps it was always fated to come to this . . .

Tom always saw himself as the cleverest of us all . . . of us all . . .

"Of course!" he exclaimed aloud.

He had seen the resemblance — the thin, wide mouth, the lean face, the long limbs, the mocking smile — seen it with his own eyes! But at the time he had not made the connection. He had not realized . . .

Barda and Jasmine were staring at him. Ava's smile was fading.

Lief wet his lips. "I think Tom felt he had no choice but to help us, Ava," he said. "He felt he owed it to us. Somehow he learned that we had fallen foul of his brother — and yours. The man we know as Laughing Jack."

Jasmine and Barda gasped. Ava's shoulders stiffened beneath the feathered cloak.

"That man is no brother of mine," she rasped.

"I think he is," Lief said. "The likeness is — "

"Jack, Tom, and I are of the same blood, that is true," Ava broke in harshly. "As children at home on the Plains we were very alike to look upon, it is said, and our minds could link as though we were three parts of a whole. But when we grew old enough, we went our separate ways to seek our fortunes. Tom went not so far. I went very far, to the sea where I had always longed to be, though I could not see it with the eyes of the body . . ."

Her voice trailed off.

"And Jack?" Lief prompted softly.

"Jack went . . . farthest of all." Ava's white lips

were trembling. She made an obvious effort to firm them, and went on rapidly.

"Long ago Jack made choices that parted him from me — and from Tom — forever. That is why I say he is no longer our brother. Now and then fragments of his thoughts still whisper like evil ghosts in the dark corners of our minds. He is still part of us. But he is our enemy."

"He is our enemy, too, Ava," Lief said softly. "And the greater Enemy he calls his master is trying to destroy our land. Please help us! Lend us your boat!"

"And if I do, where will you take it?" Ava asked. She waited for Lief's answer, her head tilted to one side, her mouth a straight, hard line.

It is a test, Lief thought. *She has seen or guessed where we want to go. She is waiting to see if we will lie to her.*

"We must go to the Isle of the Dead," he said firmly.

"So, you have decided to trust me," Ava murmured. She sank back in her chair, folding her hands beneath her cloak. The Peppermint Fancies slipped from her lap and fell to the ground, but she did not seem to care or notice.

"Very well," she said. "Then hear what I say. No boat can land on the Isle of the Dead. The sea churns around its rocks like milk boiling in a cauldron. To reach the Isle, you must go first to the scarlet island and cross by the rock bridge."

"It sounds almost too easy," Barda said.

Ava raised her head. The silk band that bound her eyes gleamed in the firelight.

"The journey to the Isle may be easy," she said slowly. "But the Isle itself is another matter. I can tell you nothing of it — except that no one who has set foot upon it has ever returned. If you value your lives you will forget it, and go on your way."

A cold knot tightened in Lief's stomach as she smiled.

15 - The Scarlet Island

An hour later, Lief and Barda were rowing Ava's tiny, battered boat across the channel that lay between the mainland and the scarlet island. The channel was rough, and wider than it had first appeared. They were still only halfway to their goal, and though the tide was with them, the work was hard.

Spray beat on them from every side, and for once they were glad of the stiff oiled coats they had taken from the fishing hut in Broome. Choppy water slapped against the blunt stern where Jasmine sat with Filli chittering unhappily beneath her collar. Kree flew overhead, the only one who was dry.

Finding that her guests were determined to make their journey, despite her warnings, Ava had shrugged and told them to take the boat if they wished. They would find it by the water, she said, tied to a post.

The hire fee, she had added coolly, was five gold coins. And for an extra gold piece she would store their packs until they returned, for the boat was too small to take extra weight. In silence she had held out her hand, her lips moving as Jasmine counted the coins into her gloved palm.

"Robbery!" Barda growled now, as he bent over the oars, water streaming from his cap, hair, and beard. "Even if I had not known the woman was Tom's sister, her outrageous prices would have made me suspect it. Five gold coins for a boat that is barely seaworthy! And one for keeping our belongings!"

"It does not matter. There is still a great deal of gold in the bag the Dread Gnomes gave us," called Jasmine, who still cared no more for money than she had when she lived in the Forests of Silence. "Besides, Ava no doubt expects us to die on the Isle. She thinks she has seen the last of her boat."

And indeed, as it turned out, Ava's boat was destined never to return to its owner. Just past the center of the channel, the companions suddenly found themselves ankle deep in water.

Ragged holes had appeared in the boat's hull, and water was pouring in. Jasmine snatched up a small bucket and began to bail frantically. Lief and Barda redoubled their efforts, gritting their teeth and pulling with all their strength.

The boat drew closer, closer to the island. But every moment the holes in the hull were opening wider, and despite all Jasmine's efforts the water was rising.

The boat began to settle. Waves lapped over the sides. Filli shrieked piercingly.

"We are in for it, I fear!" Barda said grimly. "Lief — we seem to be making a habit of this. Pull your oar free and use it to keep afloat. I will take care of Jasmine."

Lief did not argue. Barda was a far stronger swimmer than he was.

In minutes they were floundering in freezing water.

Again! Lief thought desperately. Clinging to the oar, he shook the wet hair out of his eyes and looked around for Jasmine and Barda.

He saw their heads bobbing just ahead of him. Barda was swimming strongly, pulling Jasmine with him. Filli was clinging in silent terror to Jasmine's hair. Kree was flying above them, screeching encouragement.

The tide will aid us, Lief told himself, beginning to paddle slowly forward. *And this time it is day. This time we can see the shore. And Barda and I are practiced at surviving in the sea, after all.*

The last thought made him smile, even as his teeth chattered with cold. How strange and ridiculous that his and Barda's ordeal beyond Bone Point might be the very thing that saved them now.

And just at that moment, something made him look over his shoulder.

Far away across the water, Ava's towering sign gleamed in the sunlight. But Lief could not see the cottage beneath the sign, or the waves foaming at the tip of the point.

His view was blocked — blocked by a dark ship with a broken mast and the rags of sails fluttering in the wind. Silently the ship rocked at anchor about halfway across the channel.

The Lady Luck. Waiting.

In terror, Lief turned, cast aside the oar, and struck out wildly. Fear gave strength to his arms and banished the cold that might otherwise have slowed him. His eyes fixed on the red blur ahead, he plowed through the water, using the waves as he had learned to do, thinking of nothing but flight.

And sooner than he would have believed possible he was clambering onto dry land and falling, panting, beside Barda and Jasmine into a dense, fragrant mass of scarlet lilies.

✳

Barda and Jasmine could not see *The Lady Luck* when they turned to look for it after Lief had blurted out his story. Lief could no longer see it, either. But the ruby in the Belt of Deltora was palest pink, signalling danger. Lief knew the ship was there. Visible or invisible, it was there, anchored in the channel.

Barda groaned and ran his hands through his wet hair.

"I sighted the cursed ship, too, when we had almost reached Ava's shop," he admitted reluctantly. "It was moving towards the point then. I thought my mind was playing tricks."

"As I did, when I first saw it," Lief muttered, clambering to his feet. "But it was no illusion, Barda. *The Lady Luck* has followed us. It has followed us all the way down the coast." His stomach churned at the thought.

Barda, too, looked sick.

Jasmine glanced uneasily from one to the other. "Let us move on," she said, jumping up quickly and tugging at Lief's arm. "It would be better, perhaps, to be away from the sea."

They began walking, carefully threading their way through the tall, bloodred flowers that seemed to grow thickly all over the island, clothing it in a rich mantle of scarlet.

The lilies bent and swayed around them, black-fringed petals cool and fleshy, golden stamens leaving trails of golden pollen wherever they touched. Not far ahead, rising high on the far side of the island, was the rocky outcrop that marked the beginning of the archway. Beyond that was the diamond brilliance of the Isle of the Dead.

But Lief hardly noticed his surroundings. His

mind was still on the specter of *The Lady Luck*. Nervously he glanced over his shoulder and as he turned back he saw that Jasmine was watching him in concern. He suspected that she thought he and Barda had been seeing visions.

"We are not imagining this, Jasmine!" he snapped. "The ship is real! You searched for us for over a week, and you could not find us — even in your dreams! Yet we were on the ship, within Deltoran waters, all the time."

"I know this!" Jasmine shook her head. "But how could the — the crew — have known what happened to you after you jumped overboard? How did they know where to find you?"

"Somehow they must sense us," Barda muttered. "Somehow . . ." Suddenly he stopped, his face alert.

"The gold piece!" he hissed. "Lief! You won two gold coins when you played that game, but you only returned the one you had borrowed. Perhaps . . ."

Lief dug deep into his pocket and pulled out the gold coin he had won after playing the beetle game.

"Throw it away!" Barda urged. "Throw it into the sea! Perhaps, once we are rid of it, the ship will cease haunting us."

"If you throw it into the sea, it will be lost forever," Jasmine hissed. "Who knows what will happen then?"

She held out her hand impatiently. "Give the coin to me, Lief! I am unknown to the crew of *The Lady*

Luck. I owe them nothing! I have never set foot on their accursed ship."

Lief hesitated, then handed over the coin. Nodding with satisfaction, Jasmine put it away in the Dread Gnomes' money bag.

"There," she said, returning the bag to her jacket pocket. "Now, let us concentrate on what is to come. The guardian of the Sister of the West no doubt awaits us on the Isle of the Dead. We must — "

She broke off with a startled cry as Kree suddenly swooped at her head and wheeled away, screeching. Filli, clinging to her shoulder, gave a high, despairing squeal.

A curious expression crossed Jasmine's face. She looked down and her eyes widened in horror.

Puzzled and alarmed, Lief and Barda looked down, too. But there was nothing to be seen — nothing but nodding scarlet lilies, trembling golden stamens, a few green leaves, and the deep, soft earth beneath.

"Beware!" Jasmine shrieked. She began to kick and stamp violently. Lilies toppled and fell around her, crushed beneath her feet. She bent amid the ruin of the flowers and began brushing wildly at her legs.

Lief and Barda gaped at her. What had come over her? They could see that the dull cloth of her leggings was bright with smears of golden pollen beneath a clinging mass of lily petals. But what did that matter? Where was the danger in . . . ?

And then they saw the blood — the blood dripping from Jasmine's hands, the blood soaking her leggings, running down into her boots. And they saw that the black fringes of the swollen "petals" she was clawing from her legs were wriggling. They saw feelers like golden stamens twitching angrily and razor-sharp pincers snapping as they were dragged from raw wounds.

The things clinging to her are not lily petals, Lief thought, numb with shock. *They look exactly like them, but . . .*

"Beware!" Jasmine shrieked again, still tearing the creatures from her legs. "Lief! Barda! They are on you, too! They are — eating us alive!"

16~ Blood and Bone

The next moment Lief and Barda, too, were stamping, kicking, shuddering as they plucked from their bodies the hundreds of scarlet petal-shaped horrors that had cut through their clothes, then begun gnawing at their flesh.

Lief's hands were slippery with blood. His head was spinning. As fast as he tore the creatures away, others were attacking, crawling up from the trampled lilies beneath his feet, slipping silently from the stems that nodded all around him.

His blood ran in streams into the rich earth, and it seemed to Lief that the lilies around them trembled with pleasure as they drank.

He felt disgust, horror, fear. But he felt no pain. Dizzy and unbelieving, he watched as a red creature fastened itself to his wrist and bit deeply. Blood flowed over the smears of yellow pollen that marked his skin. He pulled the creature off. A scrap of his flesh tore away with it, but he felt nothing at all.

It is the pollen, he thought hazily. *The pollen numbs the skin. That is why we did not realize what was happening. The lilies shelter the creatures and prepare their victims. The creatures' leavings feed the lilies. It is a partnership. A horrible partnership . . .*

He stared, revolted, at the flowers around him, seeing them properly for the first time. He saw the scarlet petals fringed with black, the cluster of trembling stamens in the center, heavy with pollen.

Blood lilies. Blood lilies . . . and fleshbanes.

The names floated into his mind quite suddenly. And with the names came a picture — a vivid painting of scarlet flowers. For some reason the memory made him think of the library in Del. The library . . .

And suddenly his face burned as he realized that he had seen the painting in Josef's book — *The Deltora Book of Monsters*. But he had read none of the text except the title.

Leafing quickly through the book so as to be able to tell Josef that he had read it, he had not even noticed the creatures that Josef had no doubt shown camouflaged among the lily flowers.

Fool! he told himself savagely. *If you had taken the time to read the words you would have known the blood lilies were on this island. You would have known of the fleshbanes. You would have been warned —*

Why did Ava not warn us?

The question pierced his mind like an arrow, but before he could think too much about it he became aware that Jasmine was shrieking to Barda.

The next moment Barda charged forward and, ignoring the fleshbanes still clinging to his body, began felling lilies by the dozen with great sweeps of his sword.

That will do no good, Barda! Lief thought in desperation. *The lilies may die, but the fleshbanes will live on. They will keep attacking us from below.*

He pressed his bloodstained hands to the Belt of Deltora.

"Help us!" he whispered, concentrating with all his might. "Dragon of the diamond, hear me! Help — "

His heart leaped as suddenly Barda jumped back and with a crackling roar the heap of slashed lilies burst into flames. The next moment juicy stems were spitting and hissing as they burned. Leaves and flowers were shrivelling. Fleshbanes in their hundreds were curling and dying.

Joyfully Lief looked up, searching the sky for the dragon that must at last have answered his call.

But no vast, glittering shape hovered above them. No matter how keenly he looked, he could only see Kree, swooping and screeching amid the slowly rising smoke.

Dazed with disappointment and confusion, he looked down again. Where the fallen lilies had been there was now a smoking circle of blackened earth littered with the charred bones of birds that had fallen victim to the fleshbanes in times past. And stepping onto the blackened patch, grinning in triumph, was Jasmine, the jar of fire beads clutched in her hand.

In seconds she was wreathed in steam as her wet boots sank into the hot ground. As Lief watched, she took more beads from the jar and threw them violently into the lilies ahead of her.

Flames leaped upwards. The lilies caught fire, burning like torches, then collapsing into piles of soggy ash. The blackened patch lengthened.

Lief stumbled into the center of the burned ground with Barda close behind him. Safe from further attack at last, they tore the remaining fleshbanes from their skin and crushed them into the steaming earth.

"I think we have enough fire beads to clear a path to the other side of the island," Jasmine panted, turning back to them as Kree landed on her shoulder with a triumphant squawk. "But it will be a near thing. The lilies are damp and the fire will not spread."

"That may be just as well," Barda said. "It would be a pity for us to escape being eaten alive only to be burned to cinders."

He looked ruefully down at his blood-soaked leggings. "I think we should try to stop this bleeding before going on."

Jasmine nodded quickly, crouched on the scorched ground, and began pulling balm and bandages from one of her bulging pockets.

"I cannot believe that none of us felt those creatures attacking!" she said, passing bandages to Barda. "If it had not been for Kree seeing what was happening from above, we would have been lost — staggering from loss of blood, unable to escape."

She glanced at Lief and her face changed. "Sit down, Lief!" she said abruptly. "Put your head between your knees. You are pale as a ghost."

"I am all right," Lief muttered. "I mean — I am not faint, only worried. When we were most in danger, I called the diamond dragon. It did not come."

"It is on its way now, no doubt," Barda said. "Never fear, it will be with us by the time we reach the other side of the island."

"If we *do* reach it," Jasmine said grimly, glancing at the lilies waving softly around them. "Those flesh-eating creatures are not going to give up. As soon as the ground cools, they — "

She broke off. She was staring along the short, blackened trail left by the fire. Lief followed her eyes and saw, in the newly burned area, something stretching across the path.

The obstacle looked like part of a huge cage. It had been scorched, but had remained standing while the lilies smothering it had fallen to ashes.

"What is it?" Barda frowned. "A fence? Could it

be that these cursed plants were once kept in a field?"

They began walking quickly along the blackened path. But as they grew closer to the mysterious barrier, their footsteps slowed. There was something very familiar about the barrier's shape. All of them had begun to have grave fears about what was ahead.

"Jasmine — more fire beads," Lief said quietly.

Jasmine bit her lip. She threw fire beads to the left and right of the blackened trail. The blood lilies on both sides of the mysterious object flared up, wilted, and at last fell to ash, revealing what in life they had hidden.

Half-buried in ash and earth was the skeleton of a vast beast with enormous fangs, huge wings, and ribs so mighty that they looked like a tall, curved fence. The beast's huge skull rested peacefully on the long bones of outstretched forelegs. Its long, spiked tail curved gently around its body.

It had died in the hollow where it lay, without a fight.

His throat aching, Lief fell to his knees beside it and gently touched one bare, curved rib. He knew that he had at last found the diamond dragon.

"The fleshbanes ate it while it slept," he muttered. "They stripped it to its bones."

"But why would it have risked sleeping here?" exclaimed Barda. "This island was part of its territory. Surely it knew — "

"Perhaps there were few blood lilies on the island then," Jasmine said soberly. "Perhaps they grew only around the margins — just enough to keep intruders away. The dragon did not count on their spreading so vastly over the centuries."

"No doubt it did not think its sleep would last so long," said Lief.

He was filled with a terrible sadness. His heart ached to think of the mighty beast sinking into enchanted dreams at the bidding of the man it called Dragonfriend, not knowing that it would never wake.

But he knew that he had no time for grief. The dragon was dead. It could not help them to destroy the Sister of the West. He bowed his head and put his hands to the amethyst on the Belt of Deltora.

Veritas! he thought fiercely. *Veritas, I need you! Come to me if you hear me. Come to me if you can!*

He felt the amethyst warm feebly beneath his fingers.

"What is that sound?" Jasmine hissed suddenly.

Lief glanced over his shoulder at her, very startled. Jasmine was frowning, bending forward. Filli was clinging to her collar, his eyes wide, his gray fur standing on end. Kree was standing rigidly on her shoulder, his head on one side. Plainly whatever Jasmine could hear, they could hear, too.

"What sort of sound?" Barda put his hand on his sword.

"A ticking," Jasmine breathed. "There."

She pointed to the huge, scorched skull. Cautiously she moved closer and bent to listen again. Then she kneeled and began scraping away earth and ash from beneath the tip of the mighty lower jaw. Kree squawked uneasily.

"Jasmine, take care!" Barda exclaimed.

But Jasmine did not even look up. By the time Lief and Barda reached her she had made a sizeable hole in the soft earth.

And now all of them could hear the ticking, tapping sound.

"It is under the tip of the jaw," Jasmine breathed, as her companions peered into the hole. "Between the bones of the forelegs. Almost as if — "

And at that moment her eyes widened. Her fingers had touched something.

Lief watched, holding his breath, as slowly she brushed the remaining earth away. And there, clasped between the long white bones of the dragon's forelegs, protected beneath the jaw, was something smooth, pale, and glittering.

It was a giant egg. And within it, something was tapping.

Carefully Jasmine eased the egg out of its hiding place. Earth and ash showered from its shining surface as she lifted it into the sunlight and wordlessly held it out to Lief.

Lief took the egg in his hands. The tapping sound stopped abruptly. For a moment there was silence. Then there was a sharp crack, and the smooth surface split from end to end.

A sharp snout forced its way through the opening. Small clawed feet scrabbled violently. The eggshell separated into halves and fell to the ground. And there, squirming in Lief's hands, was a tiny, perfect, glittering dragon, blinking in the sunlight.

17 – The Isle of the Dead

As the companions stared at the tiny beast in awe, Filli edged down Jasmine's arm, his eyes wide with curiosity. The baby dragon snapped its jaws, and Filli hastily retreated. The dragon yawned and stretched its wings. Then it made a harsh, barking sound and snapped its jaws again.

"It wants food," said Jasmine, and began feeling in her pockets.

"I cannot believe this!" exploded Barda, finding his voice at last. "How could an egg remain fresh for centuries?"

"Why not? What do we know of dragon eggs?" Lief murmured, staring at the little creature in fascination. "Plainly the shell was too thick and hard for the fleshbanes to crack. And the Belt roused the baby to hatch, as it would have roused its mother, had she lived. It is wonderful!"

"That is all very well," Barda said. "But what are we to do with it now? We cannot stay here. The flesh-banes are driven away for now, but they will be back."

The dragon barked again, baring its tiny fangs, and hastily Lief flattened his hands a little, to keep his fingers out of harm's way.

Jasmine had found some strips of dried fish and was soaking them in water from her flask.

"Put it in the pocket of your coat, Lief," she said briskly. "It will be comfortable there, near the Belt."

She lifted the flap that covered one of Lief's deep coat pockets and tipped the mess of softened fish inside.

Cautiously Lief lowered his hands until the dragon was beside the pocket, which Jasmine was holding invitingly open. The baby dragon raised its head. Its tiny forked tongue flickered in and out. It barked excitedly, then abruptly slithered into the pocket headfirst. The next moment they heard greedy chewing sounds.

"Good," Jasmine said with satisfaction. "Now we should go."

"Indeed?" snapped Barda. "With a dragon in Lief's pocket? What do you think it will do when all the fish is gone?"

Jasmine shrugged. "I imagine it will go to sleep," she said.

They skirted the diamond dragon's sad skeleton and, with Jasmine in the lead throwing fire beads to clear the way, began to move slowly forward.

The sound of the sea grew louder. The brightness of the Isle of the Dead began to fill the horizon. And at last they stepped out from among the lilies onto the narrow band of flat rock that formed the island's rim.

The archway rose in front of them, craggy and dark. Wind whistled around it. Wild water raged beneath it, churned to thick white foam. The thought of using it as a bridge was terrifying.

"Once the two islands were one, no doubt," Barda said. "The sea divided them — wearing the softer rock away till only the archway spanned the gap. Perhaps one day it, too, will fall."

"Not today, I hope," Lief said grimly.

He was not prepared for this. In his heart, he had always believed that a dragon would carry him and his companions to the Isle of the Dead.

But the dragon of the diamond was no more. In its place was a baby far too small to carry anyone. And there was no sign of the dragon of the amethyst. Veritas was still too weak to fly, it seemed.

"Lief! We must move from here," Barda said urgently.

Lief glanced behind him. Fleshbanes had begun to creep down from the lilies on either side of the burned path. Already they were seething in a great semicircle at the edge of the rock where the companions stood.

Hastily he began to climb, with Barda and Jasmine close behind him. He heard the roar of flame as Jasmine threw more fire beads down after them.

The arch began to curve over the sea. Lief flattened himself against the rock and crawled on his belly, trying not to think of the wind tearing at him, the sea roaring below.

He did not dare look up, even when he realized that he must have reached the highest point of the arch. But still he was aware of the blinding glare of the island ahead.

And evil, he thought. *Evil and malice.*

He could feel it, burning into his skin.

He began to move downwards, picking his way along, determined not to slip. And slowly he became aware of a sound mingling with the roaring of the sea — a low ringing sound, growing louder and louder, boring into his ears and his mind.

The song of the Sister of the West.

Sweat broke out on Lief's brow. His knees felt weak. But he forced himself to move on, to move towards the glaring light, towards the terrible sound.

Abruptly the slope became steeper. And then, without warning, the rough rock beneath Lief's hands and knees changed to a surface as slippery as ice.

With a shout of warning he slithered forward. He could not stop himself, could not even slow. When at last he came to a halt, he desperately rubbed his watering eyes, trying to focus. He could hardly believe what he was seeing.

He was not far from the peak of an island that looked as if it was made of shining glass. There was not a tree or a bush or a blade of grass to be seen. Every surface was hard, smooth, and slippery. Every surface blazed in the sunlight.

And every surface seemed to vibrate with the terrible, low ringing of the Sister of the West.

Lief lifted his eyes to the island's peak. A huge cave gaped there — the only dark spot in all that world of glittering light.

There was the source of the sound. There the Sister lay hidden. He knew it without question.

Slowly and carefully he stood up. He looked down and his head swam. Far below him a great mat of seaweed drifted like a blot of ink in an ocean of brilliant blue, and creamy foam swirled among the jagged rocks of the shore.

He heard voices and turned. His companions were picking their way towards him, Kree flying slowly above their heads.

Only then did Lief remember the baby dragon. With a feeling of dread he lifted the flap of his pocket and peered inside. But the banging and jolting of his slide to the island had not disturbed the baby at all. It was curled up, breathing peacefully, fast asleep.

Barda and Jasmine reached him. Both were squinting in the glare, and both looked exhausted, as though already the place was draining their strength.

No doubt I look the same, Lief thought. *And we have only just begun.*

An overwhelming wave of despair rolled over him.

"I do not know why we are here," he muttered. "Without a dragon to aid us, we cannot win. And there is no escape for us now."

Jasmine and Barda looked at each other. Then Barda took Lief's arm, turned him around, and pointed towards the ground.

Lief shaded his eyes and looked. And there he saw, not two steps from where he was standing, a flat gray stone jutting from the glittering rock. It was a warning stone very like those they had seen in the

IF YOU PASS, YOUR FATE IS SEALED.
AHEAD, PURE EVIL LIES CONCEALED.
TURN NOW, WHILE YOU HAVE LIFE AND BREATH.
FLEE NOW THIS REALM OF LIVING DEATH.

east and the north, though more pitted by the weather and bearing a different verse.

Lief turned away from the dread thing, gritting his teeth. "I am a fool!" he muttered. "Of course there would be a warning stone here, as there was in the east and the north! How could I have let it take me unawares, and cast me into despair?"

"Do not blame yourself for that, Lief," Jasmine said restlessly, glancing at the standing stone, then quickly looking away. "All along, this quest has felt different from our times in the east and the north. For one thing, we have not been troubled by the guardian of the Sister of the West — if indeed there *is* a guardian at all."

Lief made no reply. He had his own grave ideas about the guardian of the west, but he did not wish to speak of them. He did not want to think what they might mean.

Gingerly, their boots slipping dangerously on the treacherous rocks, the three edged past the grim stone and began to climb towards the peak.

It was slow and perilous work, and every moment it grew harder as the evil power streaming from the cave above grew stronger, pressing them down. Kree fluttered awkwardly ahead of them, his feathers ruffled, making no sound.

They stopped to rest on a flat rock that shone like a mirror. Her face strained and white beneath the streaks of ash and blood, Jasmine ran her hand over the glossy surface.

"It is almost as if this has been painted with something clear, like lacquer — painted many, many times," she said, plainly trying to occupy her mind with something that did not fill her with fear. "I am sure there is ordinary rock deep beneath this surface. When you look closely, you can see it."

"Why would anyone paint rock?" Barda grunted, wiping sweat from his furrowed brow. "Jasmine, I have been thinking of what you said — about there being no guardian of the west. Has it not struck you that Ava, who was to be so helpful to us, according to her brother, nearly killed us twice?"

Barda had voiced Lief's secret thoughts. Lief's heart sank. He stared down at the blue sea crawling far below. He noticed idly that the drifting mat of seaweed that had looked like an inkblot was gone, and wondered what had become of it.

"First, Ava gave us a boat that sprang mysterious leaks in the middle of the channel, so we nearly drowned," Barda went on. "Then she sent us to the scarlet island without breathing a word of the flesh-eating horrors that infest it."

Jasmine frowned.

"Indeed," Lief said reluctantly. "I fear we must accept it. Either Ava is not what Tom thinks she is, or — "

"Or Tom himself is as much a servant of the Shadow Lord as his brother and sister," Barda broke in heavily. "And to me this seems the more likely. Ava let slip that all three of them share minds. Surely, if she had joined Jack on the dark side, Tom could not help but know it."

He was right. Lief knew that he was right. But he did not want to believe it. With all his heart, he did not want to believe it!

Jasmine's eyes darkened. "If Ava is the guardian of the west, then she must sense we have reached the Isle," she said. "And that means — "

Suddenly Kree screeched — screeched wildly, rising into the air, his beak gaping wide.

The companions scrambled to their feet in alarm.

And saw, clambering up the glittering rocks towards them, a huge, gold-brown beast with flippers for forelegs and a great mane of loose, flabby strips of skin, pimpled and mottled like seaweed.

The fins of the beast's mighty tail lashed the rock. Its thick blue tongue, furred with bristles, lolled from its cavernous mouth. Where it crawled, it left a trail of silver slime, glistening in the sunlight.

Its tiny eyes looked up at the companions, burning with fury. Its terrible mouth opened wider, and it roared.

"Climb!" Barda bellowed. "Climb for your lives!"

18 – The Sister of the West

U p, up they climbed, hands grasping frantically, feet sliding and slipping. But the beast was close behind them, heaving its vast body effortlessly over the shining rock. Its roars were thunderous in their ears. The smell of it — the dank odor of the sea — filled their nostrils. Again and again its long, bristled tongue shot out, slapping at their heels.

"It is sorcery! Ava — in another form!" Barda shouted.

"No," Lief panted. "It was in the sea — as we approached Ava's shop. I thought — it was seaweed. Ava was inside then — sitting by her fire."

Kree was diving at the monster's head, snapping and screeching, golden eyes ablaze. But the beast was paying no attention. It did not try to snatch Kree from the air, did not falter for a moment. Its rage-filled eyes were fixed on those who had dared to set foot on its territory, who had dared climb its rocks, glazed by the hardened slime of centuries.

The companions' chests were aching. Their minds were blurred by pain and fear. Above them loomed the darkness of the cave, and from it streamed the evil power that every moment weakened them.

At the cave mouth the chase would be over. At the cave mouth they would have to turn and fight.

But they could not win. They all knew it. The song of the Sister of the West would beat them to their knees. The rage of the beast would overwhelm them.

Lief hauled himself up onto the broad ledge that lay before the cave. He heard Barda and Jasmine clamber up beside him. He struggled to rise, fumbling for his sword.

His eyes dimmed. He could hardly see. Again he tried to get to his feet, but a great weight seemed to be pressing him down.

The monster was bellowing just below him. He could hear its vast body, its trailing mane, slapping on the rock. He tried to draw his feet back, imagining the long blue tongue curling around his ankle, pulling him down.

Then Jasmine screamed.

Lief thrilled with pure terror. He struggled to his knees, then to his feet, and his sword was in his hand.

Wind tore at his hair and beat on his face. Wildly he looked around for Jasmine.

And she was standing beside him. She was standing there unharmed, her dagger raised, her hair flying around her head, eyes wide with shock.

For below, a battle was raging. The mottled beast had reared up, its vast body rigid, the fleshy strips of its mane swollen and whipping around its head, its terrible teeth bared. And clawing at it from the air, great purple wings blocking out the sun, purple fire belching from snarling jaws, was Veritas, the amethyst dragon.

At first it seemed that the monster's death was certain. How could any beast of land and sea, however vast, however savage, defeat a dragon?

But Veritas was weakening. Lief could see it — see it in the dimming of the purple scales, the ragged beat of the leathery wings. The flight from the Sleeping Dunes had nearly exhausted what little strength the dragon had. And the monster was defending its territory. Its rage was terrible.

He watched in terrified suspense as Veritas lurched downward, talons spread.

The monster's tongue lashed out, curled around the dragon's leg, and jerked backward. Wings beating vainly, the dragon fell, crashing to the rock. And then the beast was upon it, teeth like knives tearing savagely at the pale, exposed underbelly.

The dragon roared. Flame gushed from its mouth and seared the monster's mottled hide. The monster lifted its head and bellowed its pain and fury, dragon's blood dripping from its jaws.

Then the dragon was twisting away from it, launching itself awkwardly into the air. Blood streaming from its terrible wound, it rose higher, higher. The beast below reared up, but could not catch it.

Lief, Barda, and Jasmine fell back, beaten by the wind of mighty wings as the massive purple shape rose, rose to hover beside them, then dropped heavily to the ground in front of the cave.

The song of the Sister of the West rang on, mingling with the bellows of the beast.

Slowly the companions crawled to their feet. "Lief, see to the dragon," Barda rasped. "It is all that can save you now. We will defend . . . for as long as . . ."

He could not finish. He was swaying. His sword hung from his hand as if it was too heavy for him to lift. But still he stood facing attack, and Jasmine stood with him, though her eyes were blank and her shoulders sagged.

Lief staggered to the dragon's head, fell to his knees beside it, and pressed his cheek to the dimming scales of the neck. With all his might he willed the strength of the amethyst to flow through his body and into the wounded beast.

He could hear the beat of the dragon's mighty

heart. His own heart leaped as he saw the faded scales brightening.

The voice of Veritas whispered in his mind.

Where is the dragon of the diamond?

"The dragon of the diamond is dead," Lief said.

Ah . . .

Lief looked back to where Barda and Jasmine stood together, bowed by the evil power of the cave.

The beast still had not reached them. It was raging just below, lunging upwards, then falling back, wallowing in a mess of dragon's blood and its own slime.

Why does it wait? Lief thought in amazement.

"The evil in the cave holds it back," hissed Veritas, as though he had spoken aloud. "It will force its way up here at last, but it will not enter the cave. There we will be safe."

The massive body quaked, and Lief realized with astonishment that the dragon had laughed.

"Safe! Ah, that is a great joke," Veritas snorted. "Dragonfriend would have liked that. Move aside!"

Lief moved hastily out of the way. As the dragon heaved itself to its feet he saw that the wound on its belly had closed. The long tear was still raw and red, but the blood had ceased to flow.

Jasmine and Barda turned. Lief beckoned urgently and they began stumbling towards him.

The mottled beast below them roared in rage. It reared, and with a mighty effort threw itself upwards.

But it was too late. By the time it reached the place where its enemies had stood only moments before, they had gone — gone where it could not follow.

The darkness of the cave had swallowed them up.

✳

At first Lief could see nothing, but gradually he realized that the cave was dark only in contrast to the blinding light outside. Slowly he began to make out the shape of the dragon, the shapes of his friends, and the walls of a huge cavern shrouded in spiderweb.

The floor beneath his feet was thick with dust, but beneath the dust it shone like the rocks outside. Once then, long ago, this cavern had been the den of the monster of the Isle — the same beast now bellowing outside, or that beast's ancestors.

Lief's ears throbbed with the sound of the Sister of the West pulsing from the back of the cave.

But he could hear the dragon, too. The dragon was close beside him. He could hear its heart beating. He could hear its hissing breath.

Behind him, his companions stumbled and groaned.

Lief wet his lips. "Jasmine. Barda. Come no farther," he said, his voice a croak he hardly recognized as his own. "The dragon and I will go on alone."

Neither Barda nor Jasmine replied. But still they followed him.

Step by painful step they struggled on. Every step was an effort. Every breath was pain.

Lief's sword was in his hand, but he doubted he could lift his arm. It was as if the Sister's song had penetrated every bone, every muscle of his body, poisoning his blood, spreading an aching weakness.

Then suddenly the end of the cave was in sight.

Lief's skin crawled. A dim shape hunched there. A dim, pale shape that was the source of the sound, the source of the evil, the source of the poison.

He forced himself forward, bracing himself against what he might see.

Then he felt the dragon shudder. He heard the dragon's heart begin to thunder in its chest.

And he saw what the pale shape was.

It was a man, sitting on a carved throne of stone — a man so ancient that he seemed almost transparent. A long white beard trailed down his chest. Long white hair fell to his waist. His rough garments were gray with age and dust. A spiderweb floated about him. It netted his gaunt face, sealed his eyelids, and covered the bone-thin hands that rested on the arms of his throne.

But he was alive. Shallow breaths stirred the white threads that spanned his withered lips.

And the Sister of the West was inside him. From the frail chest, pure evil poured.

Lief's head was roaring. He could not breathe.

He heard the sound of Barda's sword clattering to the ground behind him.

The man's eyes opened beneath the veil of web.

The hazy gray stare fixed on Lief for a moment. Then it drifted away, to rest on the dragon. Web threads broke and drifted as the pale lips parted. The voice came, like dead leaves rustling.

"Veritas."

The dragon was quivering all over.

"Doran," it hissed.

Lief's heart seemed to leap into his throat. Suddenly his mind was burning with the memory of the Shadow Lord's evil, gloating voice.

The upstart has the fate he deserves . . .

With horror such as he had never known, Lief stared at the ancient, tormented being on the throne.

So this had been the fate of the upstart, the one who had dared to try to foil the plan of the Four Sisters. This had been the punishment of Doran the Dragonlover. Enslaved by the Shadow Lord's sorcery, he had been condemned to centuries of half-life as the guardian of the very evil he had tried to destroy.

The gray eyes moved to meet Lief's. The lips opened. And again came the faint, rasping voice.

"You — wear the Belt of Deltora. You — are the king."

"Yes," Lief said. "I am Lief, son of Endon and Sharn, heir of Adin." It was hard to speak. The power of the Sister of the West was beating him down. But his heart was aching with pity and rage equally as he gazed into those suffering eyes, and he made himself go on. "And you are Doran the Dragonlover, beloved by the tribes of the underworld, savior of the dragons of Deltora. The one whose map led me here."

Doran's eyes flickered. A tiny spark seemed to leap within them.

"The Four Sisters . . ." he whispered.

"Only two remain," Lief said. "The Sisters of the West and of the South."

"The Sister of the West is within me," rasped Doran. "Kill me and destroy it, as I could not."

"No!" groaned Veritas. "No, Dragonfriend!"

The gray eyes warmed. The dry lips curved into a smile.

"This is not life, but living death, my friend," Doran said gently. "To me, true death would be the greatest gift. Would you deny me?"

The dragon bowed its head.

"I will die knowing that my life was not in vain," Doran murmured. "I will die knowing that the Enemy may be at last defeated. And I will die in happiness knowing that you live, Veritas. You and your kind . . ."

His voice trailed away. His faded eyes grew puzzled. "But . . . I was forgetting," he said. "This is the land of the diamond. Where is — ?"

"That dragon is dead," Veritas said stolidly.

Shadows of grief crossed Doran's ancient face. "And so, despite all, her tribe has ended," he said. "I would give much that it was not so."

Lief could not bear it. He forced his hand to his pocket and lifted out the baby dragon. It seemed to him larger and heavier than it had before.

The baby made a small, complaining sound, but did not wake as Lief held it where Doran could see it.

The amethyst dragon moved uneasily.

But Doran's face was transformed. Relief and love lit his eyes as he gazed at the small, glittering creature in Lief's hands.

"Make haste, Veritas, I beg you," he said suddenly. "Give me your gift . . . in this moment . . ."

The dragon of the amethyst bent forward.

"Farewell, Doran," it said softly. "I will see you again, in the place above the clouds. There we will be young, and we will fly together once more."

"Veritas, my true friend, we will," said the man.

The dragon moved closer, bending its neck till its head masked the figure on the throne. It paused for a moment, then drew a deep, shuddering breath.

And when it moved back, Doran's face was peaceful, like a face that was sleeping, and the gossamer threads around his mouth no longer stirred.

"What — ?" Lief heard Jasmine choke.

"He is gone," whispered the dragon. "I took his breath, as he wished."

Freed at last from its bondage, the ancient body

on the throne began to crumble. A few coins, a silver flask, and a strange, many-colored stone rolled to the ground as Doran's garments, hair, flesh, and bones fell to dust. But the horror that had been concealed within him remained.

There on the carved rock, revealed at last, was a rippling, jellylike thing, creamy white and veined with pink and gray.

Malice streamed from its shapeless form, and its song was poison, hatred, doom, and despair.

The Sister of the West.

19 ~ Vows

The dragon roared, and in that thunderous sound was all the rage, grief, and hatred of its aching heart. Fire gushed from its snarling jaws, and the soft thing on the rock throne writhed and shrank as violet flame engulfed it.

Pressed hard against the dragon's leg, the diamond baby sheltered in the crook of his arm, Lief gripped the amethyst. In a daze of heat and fear, he felt the ancient power of the gem flow through him, pouring strength into the beast.

Again Veritas roared, and again, till the throne was a bath of purple fire. The shapeless thing in the fire darkened and smoked. The veins netting its surface swelled. The low ringing sound faltered, then rose to an ear-splitting screech.

Lief screwed his eyes shut and pressed his burning face against the dragon's scales.

Abruptly, the screeching stopped. The dragon, too, fell silent. The cavern seemed to echo with a silence that was somehow more terrible than sound.

Lief felt the beast draw a deep breath. Then he heard a long, low hissing and felt a blast of white heat so intense that he fell to his knees.

There was a sharp crack. Lief opened his eyes as the hissing sound dwindled and died.

The throne had split in two. And where the Sister of the West had been, there was only a dull gray stain on the rock.

"So that is done," Veritas said soberly. "Lief, gather Dragonfriend's possessions. They must not remain here. And nor must we. Now that the evil has gone, the beast outside will claim its den once more."

Lief staggered up. The baby dragon in the crook of his arm stretched and yawned.

The flat, purple eyes blinked.

"You will never know Dragonfriend, small dragon of the diamond," Veritas said. "But your life made his last breath joyful, and so I will tell you, in times to come."

✳

In less than a minute, the dragon was bursting from the cave with Lief, Barda, and Jasmine clinging to its neck. The baby dragon had been crammed back into Lief's pocket. Filli was invisible beneath Jasmine's collar. But Kree flew below the dragon's wings, his golden eyes fixed to the ground, ready to attack.

There was no need. The beast of the Isle had retreated from the peak during the battle with the Sister of the West and was only now sliding back onto the ledge before the cave.

It roared as they escaped, but could not reach them in time to harm them. The last they saw of it, it was disappearing into the cavern, the den of its ancestors and part of its domain again at last. It had forgotten them already.

"You were right, Lief," Jasmine shouted against the rushing of the wind as they soared over the scarlet island and on across the channel. "The beast was not Ava. Ava is there — outside her shop! But what is she doing?"

Lief looked past Jasmine's shoulder. In the distance he could see Ava's feathered cloak flapping in the wind as she hurried towards the back of the shop building. Ava was carrying a large bag over one arm, and dragging three packs behind her.

"The wretch!" roared Barda. "She has sensed we escaped the Isle! She is fleeing, and taking our packs with her! She has a good boat hidden in the shed behind the house, you may depend upon it. See? The door is standing open!"

Lief could not answer. He had just seen something that Barda had not. Directly in front of them, anchored just beyond the tip of the point, was *The Lady Luck*.

Lief felt something deep within him tremble. At

the same moment he realized with dread that the dragon was losing height. It was panting with exhaustion.

"Just a little farther, Veritas!" he urged.

"I — will — try," the dragon gasped. But even as it spoke, it sank lower.

The ragged shape of the ship grew larger. Lief shut his eyes and held his breath as they passed over it.

He felt the dragon drop farther. He felt spray on his face. Then there was a hard jolt.

Lief opened his eyes on dry land. Dizzy with relief, he slid from the dragon's neck.

His companions had scrambled down before him. Both were running towards Ava, shouting at her to stop.

Lief was seized by a terrible sense of foreboding.

"Barda! Jasmine! No!" he called. But they did not hear him. He glanced at Veritas and knew that the dragon could not help him. It lay where it had fallen, eyes tightly closed.

Lief began to run. In horror he saw Jasmine reach Ava and catch at her arm. He saw Ava swing around. He saw the glint of steel.

And in seconds Jasmine was off the ground, a bony arm around her neck, the point of a knife pressed to her throat.

The movement had been all too familiar. With sick terror Lief saw the feathered hood fall back.

The face revealed was powdered dead white to the lips. Long brown hair whipped in the wind. But the black silk band no longer covered the eyes.

And those blazing, hollow eyes were the eyes of Laughing Jack.

"Keep back, or the girl dies!" he snarled.

Lief and Barda stopped in their tracks.

Filli darted from beneath Jasmine's collar and bit the man's wrist. At the same moment the point of Kree's sharp beak struck his head.

But Laughing Jack did not flinch. Perhaps he had not even noticed the attacks. For now Lief could see the heavy sweat of panic that was dissolving the powder on his face and causing the dye to run from his hair.

The man was terrified. And this made him more dangerous than ever.

"Let her go, Jack!" Lief shouted. "Let her go, and we will let *you* go, to run and hide where you will!"

From the boathouse came the sound of horses rearing and neighing shrilly.

Jasmine cried out and began to struggle. The bony arm tightened around her throat, and blood ran from beneath the point of the knife.

"Let her go, Laughing Jack!" Lief shouted again, willing Jasmine to keep still. "You have no time to waste here with us. Your evil master ordered you here to make doubly certain we would die before we even set foot on the Isle of the Dead. You came, despite your fear of this coast, because you had failed him in the north and you had to win back his favor."

Laughing Jack's eyes burned, but he said nothing.

Lief pressed on. "But now you have failed the Shadow Lord yet again. The Sister of the West is destroyed, and soon he will know it. If he finds you, nothing can save you!"

The hollow eyes suddenly widened, and Lief's stomach turned over as he saw flickering within them a spark of hope.

"I have a bargain for you, king," Laughing Jack snarled. "The life of your little comrade for the Belt of Deltora — the one thing that may save me yet."

Lief hesitated. Then he bowed his head as if in defeat and unfastened the Belt. He placed it on the ground and stepped back.

"Very well," he muttered. "Take it. Only let Jasmine go."

His heart sank as Laughing Jack shook his head.

"Oh no," the man sneered. "Do you think I am a fool to be taken in by that trick? I know I cannot touch that cursed Belt without harm."

He took a step back, pulling Jasmine with him. With his free hand he felt behind him, into the boathouse. Finding what he was looking for, he jerked viciously.

With a clatter of hooves the four black horses came slowly into view, dragging the heavy wagon behind them. Jack cursed them and heaved again at the bridle of the one closest to him until the wagon was fully out of the shed.

Dragging Jasmine to the back of the wagon, he flung open the door. He pulled out what looked like a bundle of rags and threw it to the ground at his feet.

The bundle moaned. In horror Lief saw that it was a thin woman, cruelly bound and shivering with cold. Her face was powdered to a deathly paleness. Her tangled hair was brown. Her sightless eyes were gleaming white.

"My worthless sister, Ava," snarled Laughing Jack. "It was because of her that I was ordered to come here, and make sure my brother Tom knew of it. My master knew Tom would get word to you, and try to help you through Ava. Tom has always felt responsible for my doings, however he pretends otherwise."

He gave a sneering laugh.

"Tom played into my hands to perfection! What use was Ava's famous gift when she felt my approach? She could not protect herself from me. And so I took her place. Dressed in her loathsome garments, I waited for you to come to me. In her name I gave you the advice that should by rights have sent you to your deaths!"

"But your plan failed, Jack," whispered the woman on the ground. "I saw it would be so. I warned you — "

Laughing Jack silenced her with a vicious kick.

He had not taken his eyes from Lief, and now his mouth stretched into the familiar death's-head grin.

"I kept Ava alive in case she could be of use to me," he said. "And now, it seems, she can. Put the Belt around her waist. She will carry it — until I reach a place where I can dispose of her, and rid myself of two nuisances at one time and earn back my master's favor."

"Beware, brother," muttered Ava, her white eyes gleaming. "The path you are treading leads to ruin. I see death and decay around you."

"Indeed?" sneered Laughing Jack. "Save your party tricks for those who they impress, my dear sister."

Lief felt deathly chill. He glanced at Barda's face, set hard as iron. He looked into Jasmine's eyes, bright as green fire. Then he met Laughing Jack's hollow glare.

"You cannot win, James Gant," he said softly.

Laughing Jack flinched. "Do not call me by that name," he snarled.

"That was the name you used when you tried this trick before, long ago," Lief went on, still in that same soft, level tone. "Remember what happened then, and know this. I will no more give you the Belt of Deltora than Red Han would put out the Bone Point Light. And Jasmine will not ask me to betray my people, any more than Verity would ask her father to betray his trust."

Laughing Jack's grin had gone. Hair dye mixed with sweat ran down his face, making dark tracks through the white powder that masked his face.

"Remember the lesson you learned at Bone Point," Lief said, holding his gaze. "There are some things that people of honor will not do, no matter what you threaten." He picked up the Belt and fastened it again around his waist.

For a moment Laughing Jack simply stared. Then he spat.

"So be it," he sneered. "Then if I cannot have the Belt of Deltora, I will exchange the life of the girl for safe passage away from here. You say you are people of honor. If that is true, you will not follow me, wherever I may go."

"We will not," Lief said grimly, ignoring Jasmine's eyes, which were darting in anguish at the horses. "I swear it."

Jasmine struggled violently, ignoring the choking grip around her throat. She tore at her garments, as if trying to reach her dagger. Possessions fell from her pockets — a comb, her jar of balm, and, with a soft chinking sound, the Dread Gnomes' money bag.

"Ah," breathed Laughing Jack. He snatched up the money bag and patted it, grinning broadly.

"I think it is only fair that I am paid for my inconvenience," he announced. "So this gold is mine now. All mine."

And suddenly, everything seemed to stop.

Lief caught his breath. Jasmine's eyes burned in savage triumph.

Laughing Jack's grin grew fixed. And then his own voice came floating to him across the water, echoing through the years.

All the gold is yours, my loyal crew. . . . If I take one piece of it for my own, I myself will take to the oars. I swear it on my soul!

His face became a mask of horrified disbelief. He stared at the money bag in his hand. He screamed.

Then he was gone, and all that remained where he had stood was Ava's feathered cloak, collapsing silently onto the ground.

Shuddering, Lief swung around to look at the place where he had last seen *The Lady Luck*. The ship was still visible. It was very near. And it was no longer deserted, no longer still, no longer silent.

I hear your words, James Gant, and they will bind you . . .

The ringing voice was Verity's. The wooden figurehead was turning, turning to gaze with clear, painted eyes at the skull-faced man scrabbling on the deck in an agony of fear. And without emotion, hard as the wood of which it was made, it watched as rotting arms reached for him, and dragged him below.

20 – Old Friends

For a moment there was utter stillness. Then there was a creaking groan, and slowly the hulk of *The Lady Luck* tilted and sank beneath the surface of the sea. Great bubbles rose as it slipped into the depths, and as it disappeared Lief saw that the prow was empty. The figurehead had gone.

He heard a strange mixture of sounds behind him — a whispering sound like sand falling, the snorting of horses, the clattering of hoofs, and Jasmine's loud squeal of joy.

And when he turned to look, he saw that the wagon had fallen into dust, and three horses stood pawing the ground among Laughing Jack's possessions, still scarcely able to believe they were free.

Only one horse, the smallest, was still black. The second was a powerful chestnut. The last was golden, with a creamy white mane and tail. She pawed the ground and whinnied to Lief delightedly.

"Honey!" he breathed, holding out his hand to her in disbelief. "Bella! Swift! How . . . ?"

Then he shook his head. He knew that he would never find out exactly how Laughing Jack had come to own the horses the companions had last seen at the edge of the Forests of Silence. Honey, Bella, and Swift could not tell them, and the guards who had been in charge of them were all dead.

Perhaps Laughing Jack had found the horses straying. More likely a villager had caught them, and had later been forced to give them to the moneylender in payment of a debt.

It did not really matter. All that mattered was that their suffering at Laughing Jack's hands was over.

He turned to Jasmine, who was hugging Swift, her face a picture of delight. Now he knew why she had not been able to forget Laughing Jack's horses.

"You knew the horses were ours, Jasmine!" he said. "You have known ever since we saw Laughing Jack's wagon at The Funnel, on the way to Shadowgate!"

"And you did not tell us!" Barda exclaimed. He was cutting Ava's bonds and helping her to her feet, while Bella rubbed his shoulder with her velvety nose.

Jasmine shrugged. "I saw no point in making you as miserable as I was myself," she said. "We could do nothing to save the horses then."

She shook her head, her eyes darkening as she remembered.

"But I wanted to tell you. It would have been bad enough leaving any beast in slavery to Laughing Jack. But it was agony leaving our own three horses — "

Three horses . . .

Lief looked around, startled. "But there were *four*!" he exclaimed. "Where is the last?"

"Here," said a gruff voice from behind the horses.

And then, astounded, the companions saw, climbing unsteadily to his feet, a big man with a rough red beard and eyes as blue as the sea.

In that moment they understood how Laughing Jack had spent the largest part of the sorcerer's powers given to him by his evil master. He had chosen to use it for spite — revenging himself on the one man who had defied his will.

For they all recognized the man standing, swaying, before them. He was Red Han, the lost keeper of the Bone Point Light.

✳

Much later, when all the stories had been told, Bella, Honey, and Swift had been fed and stabled in the boat shed, and Red Han and Ava had fallen gratefully to sleep in Ava's cottage, Lief, Barda, and Jasmine sat with the amethyst dragon, looking out to sea. The baby diamond dragon was beside them, gobbling fresh fish for the first time in its life.

The sun was setting as Lief opened Doran's silver flask.

The flask was filled to the brim with sand. And hidden within the sand, as Lief had suspected, was a rolled scrap of parchment — the fourth and last part of Doran's map.

Lief shook his head, dumbfounded. He had been certain that the Sister of the South would be in some wild, deserted place. But it was not so. It was in the city of Del, where their quest had begun!

"No wonder poor Josef is half mad with worry," Jasmine murmured. "If he has guessed that the fourth Sister is in Del — "

"We cannot be sure that he has," Barda broke in.

"He may only have guessed that the Isle of the Dead was our third goal. According to Lief, Josef knows of the blood lilies and fleshbanes on the red island. Surely that would be worry enough."

"Josef knows where the Sister of the South is," Lief said flatly. "He has worked it out. As we could have done ourselves."

He took out the other three parts of the map and fitted them together on the rock.

"You see?" he said, pointing at each of the four Sister signs in turn. "The Sister of the East was hidden at Dragon's Nest, Deltora's most eastern point. The Sister of the North was at Shadowgate, Deltora's most northern point. The Sister of the West was on the Isle of the Dead, our most western point . . ."

"And the Sister of the South is in Del, Deltora's most southern point," Barda finished heavily. "Yes, I see. The Enemy was taking no chances. He circled the land with evil."

They sat for a moment in silence. The sky flamed as the sun slipped below the horizon.

Barda felt in his pocket and pulled out the little puzzle box. "At least I can now look at the sea without the fear of seeing *The Lady Luck* haunting us," he said.

"I do not think it ever *was* haunting us," Lief replied. "It was haunting Laughing Jack. And now it has him, forever."

He winced at the memory of those rotting hands

pulling Laughing Jack below. He took care not to look at Jasmine.

"I do not regret what I did," she said defiantly. "It was his choice to pick up the gold and claim it for himself. All I did was remember what you had told me of his oath, and make sure he saw the money bag."

"And that was very fortunate," said Barda, playing idly with the box. "If that villain had escaped, he would have taken not only our horses with him, but Red Han as well. Now the Bone Point Light can shine again. And Verity is released from the curse. She can rest in peace."

"As can Dragonfriend," the amethyst dragon murmured, rousing itself. "Yes. We have done well. It is a good ending."

"Not quite an ending for us, I fear," Lief said shortly. "We have more to do."

He glanced down at the four parts of the map lying on the rock before him. In the dimness, the Sister sign beside the city of Del seemed to writhe like a snake.

Suddenly he was tired to his bones. His exhausted brain teemed with questions for which he had no answers.

What if we fail at this, the last hurdle? he thought. *What if we have saved all the rest of the kingdom, but we cannot save our home? How could it be that the fourth Sister is in Del? Where in heaven's name can it be hidden?*

How can we even begin to find it? And why do I feel, like Josef, that there is something I am not seeing? Some further mystery . . .

Barda gave a grunt of surprise and held out the puzzle box. A third little rod was sticking out of the box's carved side.

"I have no idea what I did to make that happen!" Barda complained, tugging at the box's lid. "And look at that! Three locks undone, and *still* it will not open. Curse the thing! I should throw it into the sea!"

"If you did, you would be sorry," the dragon said shrewdly. "You would never know what was inside."

Barda snorted. But Lief noticed that he pushed the box safely back into his pocket.

Tomorrow he will try again, Lief thought. *Whatever he says, he will keep trying until all the locks are open and all the secrets are revealed. But for now he will put the problem out of his mind.*

It came to him that he should do the same. Slowly he picked up the four map fragments and put them away.

"Very good," Veritas said approvingly.

Lief looked up in surprise.

"There is a time to plan, a time to act, and a time to rest," the dragon said. "It is wise to know which is which."

Its eyes gleamed like dull purple stars in the gloom. Slowly Lief felt his tense muscles relax.

He felt the baby diamond dragon creep close to him, and curl itself to sleep as near to the Belt as it could.

Tonight is the time to rest, he thought. *Tomorrow is the time to plan. After that — we will go to Del. And there, where this all began, it will end.*

Then he thought no more, but only sat watching the empty sea, while the quiet night fell.

∞ DELTORA ∞

Destroy the evil.
Dispel the shadows.

The quest continues at

www.scholastic.com/deltora

- •Read excerpts from the books.
- •Learn about the author, the illustrator, and the characters.
- •Play the Deltora games — if you dare!